MW00534396

VEGAN PASTA NIGHT

To Grandma Pauline, Grandma Alice & Uncle Jack.
Thank you for everything.

Inspiring | Educating | Creating | Entertaining

Brimming with creative inspiration, how-to projects, and useful information to enrich your everyday life, quarto.com is a favorite destination for those pursuing their interests and passions.

© 2022 Quarto Publishing Group USA Inc.
Text and Photos © 2022 Brianna Gallo

First Published in 2022 by The Harvard Common Press, an imprint of The Quarto Group, 100 Cummings Center, Suite 265-D, Beverly, MA 01915, USA.
T (978) 282-9590 F (978) 283-2742 Quarto.com

The Harvard Common Press titles are also available at discount for retail, wholesale, promotional, and bulk purchase. For details, contact the Special Sales Manager by email at specialsales@quarto.com or by mail at The Quarto Group, Attn: Special Sales Manager, 100 Cummings Center, Suite 265-D, Beverly, MA 01915, USA.

26 25 24 23 22   1 2 3 4 5

ISBN: 978-0-7603-7293-7

Digital edition published in 2022
eISBN: 978-0-7603-7294-4

Library of Congress Cataloging-in-Publication Data is available

Design: Tanya R. Jacobson
Cover Image: Anna DeMarco
Page Layout: Megan Jones Design
Photography: Brianna Claxton, except pages 4, 7, 13, 14, 46, 62, 84, 104, 132, 154, 170 by Anna DeMarco

Printed in China

The information in this book is for educational purposes only. It is not intended to replace the advice of a physician or medical practitioner. Please see your health-care provider before beginning any new health program.

VEGAN PASTA NIGHT

A MODERN GUIDE TO ITALIAN-STYLE COOKING

Brianna Claxton, *founder of plvntfood*

HARVARD COMMON PRESS

Contents

Introduction

Cooking is in my blood. Ask almost any Italian chef, vegan or otherwise, and they're sure to have many stories of cooking in the kitchen with their grandparents, parents, friends, and extended family. Culinary tradition isn't something you can forget; it becomes a part of who you are—it's the time we take to spend time with people we love and create something together.

MY STORY

I was born and raised in and around the city of Buffalo, New York. Niagara Falls was never far. I spent many weekends in the Eaton Centre and in the shops of St. Lawrence Market in Toronto. Most important: I grew up in the kitchen with my Italian grandmother, learning every recipe, every little tip, and every combination of flavors I could. During the summers, I would go to my aunt's farm outside of the city where I picked apples, harvested corn and pumpkins, and spent time with the horses they cared for. It was at this farm where I learned the importance of the quality of the foods we use when we're cooking and what it means to be connected to your food source. (What I didn't know is that all of those summers on the farm would lead to a career and to writing this book, sharing tasty vegan recipes with all of you.)

When I turned twenty, I moved to Los Angeles, pretty much as far away from Buffalo as you could get. It was there that my world opened even more, both in my ongoing education of the culinary world and in the opportunities that found their way to me. I started working in the world of professional cosmetics, working on the sets of TV shows and music videos, and even delved into special effects makeup. When Tim Curry told me that he liked my work at a convention, I thought I could die happy. Eventually, I started my own food blog to chronicle and showcase what I was cooking and decided to do what everyone else was doing—start posting about it to Instagram.

Yet my life was never easy. From a young age, I suffered through crippling anxiety, frequent dissociation, and an inability to focus that led to horrible grades in school. I cycled from anger to depression and had frequent severe breakdowns mentally, mostly due to an extremely toxic family dynamic, which meant a traumatizing childhood—and that trauma continued in other ways into adulthood. Thinking back, my good memories all go back to time spent in the kitchen with three family members who are the only good ones I had: Grandma

Pauline, Grandma Alice, and my one-of-a-kind, over-the-top gay Uncle Jack, who would sooner be caught dead than be caught without a dirty martini in hand. Many of my fondest memories center around being in the kitchen with them. They made it my safe space. They also believed in me when nobody else did, and I carry them in my heart wherever I go.

As I grew older, my mental illnesses started to come on full force and I was, unfortunately, put into more traumatic situations, which made holding regular jobs near-impossible. For those of you who follow me on social media, you'll know of my mental battles with borderline personality disorder and severe PTSD (among other mental illnesses), as well as physical battles with anemia, Hashimoto's thyroiditis, hypermobile Ehlers-Danlos syndrome, POTS, and endometriosis. While the deck sometimes feels stacked against me, cooking is something that allows me to forget about everything else and focus on what matters most to me: cooking incredible, compassionate meals. I'm so thankful for cooking and the power of social media because it has not only allowed me to connect with people who struggle like I do, but it also gives me the ability to have a career that I can be flexible with given my health.

Social media was never something I had really considered very much as an avenue for opportunity, especially in food blogging. When I started it, I didn't have any special plans for it to become something that I could do full time. I didn't expect to one day work directly with some of my favorite vegan brands, developing recipes and becoming a food photographer. Maybe one day I'll shake off the imposter syndrome I have about it all, but for now I'm excited to be sitting here, surrounded by my sleepy dogs, cats, and snakes on a Sunday afternoon, with Avril Lavigne's first album blaring on the record player. Fun fact about me—it's one of the only albums I can listen to when I'm working, second to the *Tenacious D in the Pick of Destiny* soundtrack.

Speaking of my sleepy dogs, my decision to become vegan comes from my profound love and respect for not only my own companions, but for *all animals*. I take pride when creating recipes knowing I'm not harming cows, pigs, or anyone else when we can have the same flavors and satisfaction that we get from eating meat and cheese. The bonds I've made with animals both through volunteering at animal sanctuaries and rescues and in my own home have given me a passion for veganism and animal rights that I see as being in step with my views on social justice and climate change. There's so much at stake, and I look at my own choices for what I eat as a form of everyday activism, where I choose peace (and delicious food) on my plate.

MY VEGAN KITCHEN

Oftentimes, I get asked what people should "know" about vegan cooking before they jump into it. What products should I have in my pantry/in my fridge? Do I really have to make all my own "cheese" now? Soybeans aren't bad for you, right? Yes, I still get asked all those questions and especially that last question, more frequently than I would like. Instead of focusing on what makes a good vegan kitchen, I recommend considering what makes a good kitchen and a good chef. Some questions I suggest asking yourself are: Do I have the right salts, oils, and spices to make anything that I can dream up? Am I approaching this dish with the right mindset? Am I having fun?

At the end of the day, a vegan kitchen shouldn't be any more or less difficult to create delicious dishes in than a "normal" kitchen. If anything, many dishes will take less time to make because of the straightforward, whole foods ingredients. On the other hand, with some time (and the right spices), you can take vegan cooking even further. For example, you can marinate a whole carrot in liquid smoke, smoked paprika, garlic powder, and vegetable broth. Cook it the right way, throw it on a bun, and it'll sub in for a hot dog. You could also put maple syrup, cinnamon, and nutmeg on a carrot, roast it, and it'll be better suited for a dessert. The versatility of spices means that knowing your way around a spice rack will become one of your strongest tools as a vegan chef. In this book, I'm hoping the recipes show you both the beauty of a simple vegan recipe and the delicious possibilities that are achievable when you spend an afternoon or a weekend in the kitchen.

When I started cooking vegan and putting more thought into the individual ingredients I was using, I wanted to understand everything inside and out. Let's touch on a few of my essential beliefs.

- Growing up, I was taught that sea salt was the best salt to use most of the time and that's something I still stand by. In this book, if you see a mention of salt, you can assume it's sea salt.

- I've done plenty of research on how and when to use different oils. If you're quickly sautéing something and want to add a little bit of flavor, I recommend olive oil. When you cook something over high heat, olive oil burns, so grapeseed oil is my choice for most high-heat applications.

- I never cook with extra-virgin olive oil. I believe it should be used as-is, either drizzled directly onto a dish or added at room temperature as part of recipe, as in a pesto or salad dressing.

- After years of developing recipes, I recommend buying plain, unsweetened soy or cashew milk, mainly because their fat contents are higher than most other plant milks and they don't add a strong flavor to a dish (like, say, coconut). Store-bought almond or oat milk tends to be a little too thin and sugary (even if you get the unsweetened kind).

- I recommend that you try making your own milk, regardless of the type. As a vegan, I find it's the best way to control the thickness. You can make cashew milk into a heavy cream consistency, which can be used in coffee or as a base for a pasta sauce. If you add a little more water, you can make half-and-half—good for thickening sauces or using in certain types of doughs (bread, desserts, etc.). Add even more water, and you have regular cashew milk that can be used like dairy milk.

- Making pasta by hand is one of the most intimate things you can do in the kitchen. Any time I've made pasta, there's this magical, mesmerizing quality to it (in fact, I feel like this is true even if you're watching someone else make pasta). Some people see pasta-making as this intimidating and challenging task that people learn to impress their friends, but I promise you that couldn't be further from the truth. Making fresh pasta is a must!

WHY VEGAN PASTA NIGHT?

Growing up, every Sunday meant pasta night with my entire family, where we'd make pounds of fresh pastas and often more than one sauce as well. We would watch Grandma Pauline make pasta as we snacked on the appetizers. As I got older, I found that pasta night doesn't even need to be strictly Italian—I've spent plenty of pasta nights making fresh spaetzle and pierogi with Uncle Jack and Grandma Alice, topping them with gravy and chives or caramelizing them in butter with onions. Pasta isn't just important to Italians; it's a staple of cuisines all over the world.

Once I moved to California, pasta nights ceased to exist for me. Everyone that I enjoyed them with was either far away or had passed away. Eventually, I started my own pasta night with close friends, including one of my best friends, Henry. He's an incredible chef who has worked at some of the best restaurants in the country. My favorite thing about those pasta nights was that even though he's not a vegan chef, it was a magical and fun experience for everyone involved. In my opinion, it's important to remember that even if we're vegan, we should still be learning new techniques and recipes from people who aren't vegan. (It's also important for non-vegan chefs to learn their way around a vegan kitchen.) The amount I learned from Henry was on par with almost everything else I had learned up until that point in my life. With cooking, we never stop learning new techniques, flavor combinations, or new ingredients we've never used before. Every time we cook, we learn—whether we realize it or not. I want this book to not only teach you the core elements of cooking, but I want you to feel inspired to put your own spins on the recipes in these pages. Cooking is something you should have fun with. The more you cook, the better you'll get and the more confident you will be to experiment and make recipes your own. Your intuition will be honed over time, and your skills will continue to grow and flourish.

In this book, you'll find recipes inspired by my entire journey. The Semolina Pasta Dough recipe on page 19 and *THE* Tomato Sauce recipe on page 27 come directly from Grandma Pauline. The Stuffed Banana Peppers, "My Favorite Soup," and Lasgane Bolognese (see pages 195, 179, and 89) were also staple recipes from her. I have entire chapters on making your own vegan meats and cheeses because these are areas I have explored deeply as a vegan chef and believe everyone should give it a try. It's not as hard as you think!

I hope that through these pages you discover a new favorite recipe, feel empowered to make your own cheese, start your own pasta night, or just flip through because you like looking at pretty pictures of food (I don't judge). But seriously, I worked hard on making them look as appetizing and as beautiful as I could, so I hope you enjoy it. I can't say writing this book was the easiest or best experience of my life. It really pushed my limits physically and mentally given my health, but I am proud of the recipes and photos I've created and am happy to finally show them to you all. Italian cuisine has and always will have a special place in my heart, and I think it will for you too (if it didn't already) after you make even just a few of the recipes in these pages.

Find me on Instagram (@plvntfood) and tell me your favorites! As my grandmother always said, very loudly and before anyone dared take a bite of their meatballs: "*MANGIAMO!*" (In Italian, that means "let's eat!")

All my love,

Brianna Claxton

Chapter 1

Fresh Pastas, Sauces, and Essentials

———————

Pasta Essentials: Fresh Pasta

Making fresh pasta can seem daunting. But trust me, it's so much easier than you think! You can do it the old-fashioned way, like my grandma, and work by hand. My favorite thing about that method is that you can use anything to roll it out . . . my grandma would use a wine bottle most of the time. You can also do it my way, making the dough in a food processor or stand mixer and using a pasta machine to roll it out. Either way, I promise the results are so fantastic you will be tempted to make fresh pasta every week! Making a thin, flat sheet of pasta gives you so much versatility, too. You can make pasta with a variety of thicknesses (for example: spaghetti, tagliatelle, and pappardelle), or you can turn it into farfalle, ravioli, tortellini, orecchiette, garganelli, and more! The whole point, regardless of the shape, is to have fun with it.

Growing up, Grandma Pauline would make pasta a variety of ways, including 00 flour (a very finely milled flour) with eggs, semolina flour with eggs, and a mix of those two flours with eggs. However, when she would make different shapes other than straight pasta, she would make a dough using only semolina flour and water. That dough, which you'll find on page 19, originally became my favorite not because it's vegan, but because it's a drier dough that gives you more versatility and allows you to make a larger range of shapes.

When making pasta dough, start slow and don't overwork the dough before kneading. I recommend mixing the dough until just combined before you start the kneading process. Kneading can seem like hard work, but it can be fun. My grandmother always said kneading your way to a tender dough is a good way to get your aggressions out! With kneading, if you think you have kneaded enough . . . knead more. You want a shiny, supple dough that bounces back when pressed firmly with your fingertip. Once you're done kneading the dough, you'll need to wrap it in plastic wrap and place it in the fridge to rest for about 30 minutes to an hour. Taking time to do this allows the gluten to relax and the dough to rehydrate, which makes it more pliable and tender.

To roll out the dough with a pasta machine, you'll want to start with the setting at its widest. Roll it through, fold it in half, and then repeat three times on each setting until you get to the thinnest size for your pasta. For straight pastas, I think a size 5–6 is perfect; for shaped pasta, a size 3–4 works well; and for filled pasta, a size 1–2 should give you the thin dough you need. You can add flour to keep the pasta from sticking but be careful not to add too much. For hand-rolling pasta, use a rolling pin (or wine bottle). My grandma would let part of the dough hang off the counter as she rolled, so gravity would help in the stretching and thinning process. Making pasta this way does take a lot more time than with a pasta machine, but it is fun—especially with friends and family. Kids love it! Just keep rolling until you get it as thin as you need it (which for straight pastas will be about the width of a credit card). Again, when you add flour, be careful not to overdo it.

Once your dough is ready, it's time to cut it into sheets. Make sure you generously flour between each layer. As with rolling, keep an eye on the dough. You don't want to use so much flour that you dry it out. When your sheets are ready to go, you can then turn them into whatever shape you want. There are plenty of fun pasta tools you can use to make different edges, but I was taught to use a knife and that's what I still use to this day.

With fresh pasta, you don't have to cook it as long as dried pasta from a box. You'll get a more tender bite, even at al dente, and the rustic shapes will add that little extra *something* to each dish. Pay close attention to the texture as you cook your first batch or two. For most pastas, letting them cook an extra 15 to 20 seconds past when they float is the ticket!

SEMOLINA PASTA DOUGH

This is my basic, go-to pasta dough. You can dry it, you can freeze it, you can fill it, and this recipe isn't even one that I had to convert to make vegan. It's commonly used across Italy and is vegan by default. Make sure to use semolina flour, which gives this pasta its signature slightly yellow color and provides a subtle flavor and bite to the finished, cooked pasta. This is a durable flour, making it easy to cut into any shape you want.

Yield: About 1 pound (455 g) of dough (4 servings)

Time: 1 hour

INGREDIENTS:

2 cups (360 g) semolina flour

½ cup (120 ml) plus 2¼ tablespoons (32 ml) warm water, divided

Salt to taste (I use about ½ teaspoon salt)

All-purpose or 00 flour, for flouring work surface

METHOD:

1. In a large mixing bowl, add the semolina flour and make a well in the center.

2. Add ½ cup (120 ml) of water and salt to the well and mix with a fork to combine.

3. Once the mixture turns into a shaggy dough, move it to the countertop and gently knead it for 3 to 5 minutes.

4. Form it into a smooth, compact dough ball—if the dough is too dry, then add a tiny bit of the reserved water.

5. Wrap the dough in plastic wrap and allow it to rest for at least 30 minutes, ideally an hour. Knead the dough a couple of times and roll it out onto a lightly floured surface. Use all-purpose or 00 flour to coat the surface.

6. Using a rolling pin or pasta machine, roll the dough out to ⅛-inch (3 mm) thickness. If not using a pasta machine, still keep the width to about 6 inches (15 cm) for the next step.

7. Roll the dough up into thirds, folding both sides into the middle, and then folding those sides over again.

8. Flip it over and cut into the desired thickness or leave in sheets to make other pasta shapes (see page 16).

9. After cutting to the desired thickness or making shapes, coat in all-purpose or 00 flour and place onto a baking tray. Allow to dry out for 15 to 20 minutes.

10. Cook in a large pot of boiling salted water for about 4 to 5 minutes.

FLAVORED DOUGHS

Flavored doughs add color to your dishes, and they're a fun way to utilize different ingredients. It's a sneaky way to up your presentation game or make it fun for your kids to get in on the action in the kitchen. Even the normal suspects that "hate beets" are going to want to give pink pasta a try, because . . . who wouldn't?

Yield: About 1 pound (455 g) of dough (4 servings)

Time: 1 hour

INGREDIENTS:

2 cups (360 g) semolina flour

½ cup (120 ml) plus 2¼ (32 ml) tablespoons warm water, divided

Salt to taste (I use about ½ teaspoon salt)

All-purpose or 00 flour, for flouring work surface

CHOOSE ONE OF THE FOLLOWING OPTIONS:

¼ cup (39 g) frozen spinach, thawed and drained

1 tablespoon (9 g) activated charcoal

1 tablespoon (10 g) beetroot powder

1 tablespoon (7 g) ground turmeric

METHOD:

1. Make the Semolina Pasta Dough according to the recipe instructions on page 19, but when adding the water and salt, also add flavor and/or coloring!

    a. For spinach pasta, take the thawed and drained frozen spinach and pulse in a food processor until smooth. Add that into the pasta dough.

    b. For "squid ink" pasta, add the activated charcoal in with the water and salt to the pasta dough.

    c. For beetroot pasta, add the beetroot powder in with the water and salt to the pasta dough.

    d. For turmeric pasta, add the turmeric powder in with the water and salt to the pasta dough.

NOTES:

• *You can really use any flavoring or coloring you'd like! These are just my personal favorites.*

• *If making sheets of pasta for lasagne, it's fun to mix in fresh herbs, chopped, so they're visible in the sheet of pasta. It helps build even more flavor and looks beautiful!*

GNOCCHI THREE WAYS

Potato or Sweet Potato Gnocchi

You may have tried traditional potato gnocchi, but did you know you can also make it with sweet potato or ricotta cheese? My grandmother used to call them "little Italian dumplings of love," and you can't go wrong pairing them with any type of sauce, even if it's just butter and Parmesan. Feel free to double or triple this recipe. These keep for up to 7 days covered in the fridge or up to 3 months in the freezer!

METHOD:

1. Chop the cooled, peeled baked potatoes into large chunks. Press one piece at a time through a potato ricer until there are no lumps. If you don't have a potato ricer, you can use a fork to mash the potatoes. Do *not* put them in a food processor or blender, as they will get gummy.

2. In a mixing bowl, add the flour, olive oil, salt, and mashed potatoes. Mix until combined and then knead into a ball of dough. If the mixture is too tacky, add extra flour until it doesn't stick to your hands or the bowl. If the flour will not fully mix into the potatoes, add a little extra olive oil until it comes together. The key is to avoid a wet, sticky dough. You want the dough to be easy to work with as you form it into little dumplings.

3. Keep the dough covered so it doesn't dry out, taking one small portion at a time to form into gnocchi. Take 1 teaspoon of dough and squeeze it in your fist to make a compact, roughly shaped ball, then roll it between your palms to make it round.

4. To create the traditional gnocchi shape with grooves, place a fork or gnocchi board face down on the counter. Take the ball of dough and place it at the top of the back of the fork. With your thumb on the piece of dough, slide the gnocchi down the tines of the fork until you reach the counter. The gnocchi will turn under your thumb until it has grooves going around about three-quarters of the dough and a small inset divot where your thumb was.

Yield: 8 servings

Time: 40 minutes

INGREDIENTS:

1 pound 4 ounces (459 g) baked russet potatoes, cooled and peeled (for sweet potato gnocchi, substitute the same amount of sweet potato)

2½ cups (313 g) all-purpose flour plus more as needed

2 tablespoons (28 ml) olive oil

1 teaspoon salt

5.   Repeat with the remaining pieces of dough. If the dough becomes sticky at any point, toss the shaped gnocchi with flour to prevent them from sticking together and knead a bit of extra flour into the remaining unshaped dough.

6.   To cook the gnocchi, bring a large pot of salted water to a boil. Add the gnocchi to the pot and let it cook for about 4 to 5 minutes or until the gnocchi float to the top, at which point, you should allow them to cook for an additional minute. Use a slotted spoon to scoop them out and add them directly into the sauce of your preference; you can also crisp them by frying them in hot butter.

Ricotta Gnocchi

Yield: 4 servings

Time: 30 minutes

METHOD:

1.   Add the ricotta, salt, and flax eggs to a food processor and process until smooth. Then, add the flour and pulse until combined and a dough starts to form. Remove from the food processor and knead the dough for about a minute until it comes together. It should hold together but still be moist.

2.   Transfer the gnocchi mixture to a pastry bag and place in the fridge for 10 minutes.

3.   Bring a large pot of salted water to a boil. Cut a ½-inch (1.2 cm) opening on the bottom of the gnocchi bag. Working in batches, pipe the dough into the pot, cutting off 1-inch (2.5 cm) pieces with kitchen shears or a paring knife, letting them drop into the water.

4.   Once the gnocchi float, use a slotted spoon and remove them, then add to the sauce of your choice.

INGREDIENTS:

2 cups (500 g) vegan ricotta (see page 56 for recipe)

1½ teaspoons salt

2 flax eggs (2 tablespoons [21 g] ground flax plus 6 tablespoons [90 ml] water, mix well and let it sit to thicken for 10 minutes)

1 cup (125 g) all-purpose flour

THE TOMATO SAUCE

Every Italian or Italian American family has their own special take on tomato sauce. The reason this sauce is "THE" tomato sauce is because of how ridiculously long it takes to cook. Canned tomatoes are great for making sauces because they're cheap and accessible, but they end up having a metallic flavor to them at times. The cooking process of making this sauce eliminates that and leaves you with a deeply rich, hearty sauce bursting with flavor that you'll want to put on top of everything. Some of my fondest memories with my grandmother are making and jarring this sauce. Growing up, I remember making it with her every single week and then packaging it into jars so it would be ready to go whenever we wanted it. I recommend you do the same. Make it worth the effort and double, triple, or quadruple this recipe!

Yield: 4 cups (980 g; 8 servings)

Time: 3 days

INGREDIENTS:

1 can (28 ounces, or 785 g) tomato puree

12 ounces (340 g) tomato paste

4¾ cups (1.1 L) water

¼ cup (12 g) dried oregano

¼ cup (8 g) dried basil

¼ cup (36 g) garlic powder

Salt to taste

1 teaspoon sugar

METHOD:

1. Add all of the ingredients to a stockpot over low heat. Start this process in the morning. Let it cook on low all day, stirring every hour or so to prevent burning.

    NOTE: *Low heat should be the lowest setting on your stove top! You'll see the sauce bubble a little bit eventually, but it should just be a bubble or two that goes away when you stir and it should never be bubbling rapidly. If your pan is getting so hot you're seeing steam or stuff is sticking to the bottom of the pot, you need to turn that burner down!*

2. At the end of the day, about 10 to 12 hours later, turn off the heat. Before bed, transfer the pot to the fridge.

    NOTE: *Do what you can! Even an 8-hour day of cooking should be good.*

3. The next morning, take the sauce and place it back on the stove over low heat. Repeat the above process throughout the day. Then, do it for a third day.

4. At the end of day 3, it's ready to finally package or serve!

BOLOGNESE

There's a misconception in America that Bolognese is just a ground beef and marinara sauce, when there's much more to it than that. There's a wealth of other ingredients that make this sauce special. It's the perfect sauce to put on top of regular potato or ricotta gnocchi, and it's a hearty, stick-to-your-ribs kind of sauce that you'll want to make in the winter months. (In Italy, it's the base of any good lasagne.) Plus, when cooking this sauce, your house will smell incredible. It takes a long time to cook, but it's 100 percent worth the wait.

METHOD:

1. In a large heavy-bottomed pot, add a few tablespoons (45 to 60 ml) of olive oil and brown the ground beef, season with salt and pepper. Remove and set aside on a plate, covered, until needed.

2. In a food processor, add the carrots, celery, onion, and garlic. Run on high until everything is chopped very fine, almost to a "pulp."

3. Add the remaining ⅓ cup (80 ml) of olive oil and once shimmering, add the veggie mixture plus salt and pepper to taste. Cook over medium heat for about 10 minutes until the vegetables are soft.

4. Add the tomato paste and stir to combine. Cook for 2 to 3 minutes, stirring frequently.

5. Add the bottle of Pinot noir and increase the heat to high. Bring to a boil and cook for about 5 to 10 minutes until the wine has reduced by half.

6. Take the rosemary, thyme, and bay leaves and tie them up with butcher's twine into a bundle; add that in just after the wine.

7. Add the crushed tomatoes, stir well, reduce the heat to a simmer, and cover halfway with a lid. Cook for 2 hours over low heat, stirring frequently.

8. After 2 hours, add back in the browned ground beef, along with the butter and Parmesan. Stir to combine.

9. Taste and adjust the salt and pepper level, mix well, and serve with your favorite pasta.

Yield: 4 to 6 cups (1 to 1.5 L; 8 to 10 servings)

Time: 3½ hours

INGREDIENTS:

⅓ cup (80 ml) plus a few tablespoons (45 to 60 ml) olive oil, divided

1 pound (455 g) vegan ground beef (see page 64 for recipe)

Salt and black pepper to taste

3 medium-large carrots, peeled

3 ribs celery

1 large yellow onion

8 garlic cloves

2 tablespoons (32 g) tomato paste

1 bottle (750 ml) Pinot noir

2 sprigs fresh rosemary

8 sprigs fresh thyme

3 bay leaves

1 can (28 ounces, or 785 g) crushed tomatoes

4 tablespoons (55 g) vegan butter (see page 40 for recipe)

4 tablespoons (30 g) grated vegan Parmesan (see page 51 for recipe)

ALFREDO

Here's a little-known fact: Alfredo sauce in Italy doesn't have any cream in it. Traditionally, it's made with just Parmesan and butter, but that's not the Alfredo people know and love in America. For this recipe, cashews give the Alfredo that American-style creaminess. I always dare people to make this sauce for non-vegans as a test because it's so good it's just like the "real" thing (what does that even mean anymore, anyway?). In any case, I guarantee you they'd never know the difference.

METHOD:

1. In a high-powered blender, add all of the ingredients.

2. Blend until completely smooth. Stop and stir as needed and continue blending if the mixture is not yet totally smooth.

3. Adjust the salt level to taste. For a thicker sauce, add more cashews. For a thinner sauce, add more water. It's all up to preference.

4. Serve with a favorite pasta!

Yield: About 3 cups (732 g; 4 to 6 servings)

Time: 10 minutes

INGREDIENTS:

1 cup (140 g) raw unsalted cashews

2 cups (475 ml) filtered water

2 garlic cloves

2 tablespoons (28 g) vegan butter (see page 40 for recipe)

¼ cup (30 g) grated vegan Parmesan (see page 51 for recipe)

Salt to taste

HEIRLOOM POMODORO SAUCE

People think making your own sauce from scratch is intimidating, but you can make it quickly and easily and still have a sauce that's way better than store-bought. In this sauce, drawing on fresh tomatoes instead of canned gives the sauce a level of brightness, though it will not have the richness of a sauce that uses canned tomatoes. If you really pay attention while tasting though, you'll appreciate every bite: in-season tomatoes often have a floral taste that you would completely miss out on with canned. This sauce is also surprising to the eye, since using fresh tomatoes makes it look more like a vodka sauce at first glance.

Yield: 4 cups (980 g; 8 servings)

Time: 45 minutes

INGREDIENTS:

6 Roma tomatoes

1 large or 2 small heirloom tomatoes

½ yellow onion

3 tablespoons (45 ml) olive oil for roasting

Salt and black pepper to taste (for roasting and in the sauce)

6 garlic cloves

½ cup (20 g) fresh basil

⅓ cup (80 ml) extra-virgin olive oil (see page 11)

METHOD:

1. Preheat the oven to 400°F (200°C, or gas mark 6).

2. Slice the tomatoes and onion into chunks and place on a baking sheet. Drizzle with 3 tablespoons (45 ml) of olive oil and sprinkle some salt and black pepper over the vegetables.

3. Place in the oven for 35 to 40 minutes. About 15 minutes into cooking, remove the tray and add the garlic and then continue roasting.

4. After the 35 to 40 minutes are up, set the oven to broil and let the veggies sit there for just a few minutes until they get a slight char.

5. Transfer everything on the baking sheet, including any drippings, to a blender. Add the basil and extra-virgin olive oil. Blend until smooth and then taste and adjust the seasonings.

VODKA SAUCE

Do you have a very specific childhood memory of the first time you tried vodka sauce and mistakenly thought that it got you drunk? Or if not, maybe a friend has told you this story? There's no way that it was just me! Or maybe it was, because the recipe that my grandmother taught me never actually had vodka in it because she refused to buy the stuff. (She was a wine–only kind of woman.) While that sauce was delicious, I believe that there's something special that happens chemically between the vodka and the tomatoes that creates a sweet and creamy sauce. Whether or not you pretend it gets you drunk is optional.

Yield: About 4 cups
(904 g; 6 to 8 servings)

Time: 40 minutes

INGREDIENTS:

3 tablespoons (45 ml) plus
1½ tablespoons (25 ml)
olive oil, divided

1 medium yellow onion,
diced

4 garlic cloves, minced

¼ to 1 teaspoon crushed
red pepper (to taste)

1 tablespoon (16 g)
tomato paste

⅓ cup (80 ml)
good-quality vodka

1 can (28 ounces, or
785 g) whole peeled
tomatoes

1 tablespoon (15 ml)
balsamic vinegar

Salt and black pepper
to taste

½ cup (70 g) raw
unsalted cashews

1 cup (235 ml)
filtered water

¼ cup (10 g) fresh basil

2 tablespoons (15 g)
grated vegan Parmesan
(see page 51 for recipe)

METHOD:

1. In a large sauté pan, heat 3 tablespoons (45 ml) of olive oil over medium heat. Add the onion and garlic and cook, stirring frequently, until soft, about 3to 4 minutes.

2. Add the crushed red pepper and cook for 1 minute or until fragrant.

3. Stir in the tomato paste and cook for 2 minutes and then add the vodka and continue cooking for about 1 minute.

4. Stir in the canned tomatoes, balsamic vinegar, salt, and black pepper to taste. Reduce the heat to low and partially cover the pot with its lid. Simmer for 20 minutes or until reduced by half, stirring occasionally.

5. While the sauce cooks, add the cashews, water, and remaining 1½ tablespoons (25 ml) of olive oil to a high-speed blender. Blend the mixture well until very smooth. It should have a heavy cream consistency.

6. When it's finished cooking, transfer the tomato mixture to a food processor or blender, add the basil, and purée until smooth. Return the sauce to the pan and stir in ½ cup (120 ml) of the cashew cream. Taste and add more cashew cream if needed.

7. Cook until warmed through, about 2 to 3 minutes. Stir in the Parmesan and cook until it melts and incorporates with the sauce.

8. Serve with a favorite pasta.

DREDGING STATION

Growing up, I could never remember the proper order of operations when it came to dredging things. My grandmother, in her infinite wisdom, would tell me to remember the abbreviation for February (which so happens to be my birthday month). The letters F.E.B. stand for flour, eggs, and breadcrumbs—in that order. Dredging is a process that you'll use in several recipes, from Chicken Parmesan (see page 200) to Mozzarella Fritta (see page 199). When in doubt, always remember F.E.B. and secretly wish me a happy birthday while you're at it.

METHOD:

1. Mix all of the ingredients in three separate bowls, allowing the "egg mixture" to sit for 10 minutes before using.

2. Coat the ingredient (protein, vegetable, cheese, etc.) in the flour mixture first (step 1), then into the egg mixture (step 2), and then into the breadcrumb mixture (step 3). Make sure to pat off any excess flour from step 1 and to really press the breadcrumbs into what is being breading in step 3.

3. Place on a parchment-lined plate until finished dredging before cooking.

Yield: Enough dredge for 2 recipes

Time: 15 minutes

INGREDIENTS:

FLOUR MIXTURE

3 cups (375 g) all-purpose flour

2 teaspoons sea salt

1 teaspoon black pepper

EGG MIXTURE

3 cups (700 ml) plain unsweetened soy milk

¾ cup (94 g) all-purpose flour

1 teaspoon sea salt

1 tablespoon (7 g) ground flaxseeds

1 teaspoon black pepper

BREADCRUMB MIXTURE

1½ cups (175 g) plain breadcrumbs

1½ cups (168 g) panko breadcrumbs

¾ cup (90 g) grated vegan Parmesan (see page 51 for recipe)

1 tablespoon (3 g) dried oregano

2 teaspoons garlic powder

1 teaspoon sea salt

1 teaspoon black pepper

HEAVY CREAM

Heavy cream is one of the vegan dairy products that's harder to find out in the wild. It's used in so many recipes and is consistently one of my most-requested recipes on social media. In essence, you're making cashew milk (but thicker), and the addition of olive oil is what makes this recipe special. The olive oil adds another layer of fattiness and creaminess, creating a more realistic texture when you're trying to replace dairy heavy cream in a recipe. This specific recipe won't turn into whipped cream like dairy heavy cream will, but it works for every other situation where you would need heavy cream. It's great in your morning coffee if you're looking to add a touch of luxury to your routine.

Yield: 3 cups (700 ml)

Time: 5 minutes

INGREDIENTS:

1 cup (140 g) raw cashews

2 to 3 cups (475 to 700 ml) filtered water

¼ teaspoon sea salt

1 tablespoon (15 ml) olive oil

METHOD:

1. Blend all the ingredients in a high-speed blender until smooth. Start with less water at first and add more as needed until your desired thickness is achieved.

BUTTER

Butter, but make it vegan. We're lucky that there's a myriad of vegan butter options out there now, but I highly recommend making your own! It's insanely delicious, and you get far more bang for your buck than you would if you took a trip down to your local grocery store for a tub or two. This specific butter recipe is ideal for melting, browning, using in baked goods, whipping, making compound butters, or doing anything you would do with non-vegan butter. This recipe will keep in the fridge for about 3 to 4 weeks.

METHOD:

1. In a mixing bowl, add the soy milk and rice vinegar and stir. Allow to sit for 5 to 10 minutes to make "buttermilk."

2. While that sits, melt the coconut oil in the microwave until warm, but make sure to not make it too hot!

3. To the mixing bowl with the "buttermilk" mixture, add the melted coconut oil, salt, canola oil, coconut cream, and a very tiny pinch of turmeric (for color). Whisk this well until it is smooth and pale in color.

   NOTE: *You'll probably want to whisk this by hand so as to not over emulsify. You could try using a blender or food processor, but be careful. Only blend until just combined.*

4. Pour the mixture into the preferred butter molds. Place into the refrigerator for an hour or two to set—the longer the better.

Yield: 2 cups (450 g) butter

Time: 1 hour 15 minutes

INGREDIENTS:

½ cup (120 ml) plain unsweetened soy milk

2 teaspoons rice vinegar

1 cup (235 ml) refined coconut oil

½ teaspoon salt (optional)

¼ cup (60 ml) canola oil

¼ cup (60 ml) coconut cream

NOTE: *If you can't find coconut cream at the store, you can skim the cream from coconut milk. To do this, place a can of coconut milk in the fridge overnight the day before making the butter. When you open it, the thick cream on the top is what you're scooping out and measuring here.*

Very small pinch of turmeric

NOTE:

To make whipped butter, after you have whisked the butter mixture well, put the bowl in the fridge for about 30 minutes or until it becomes slightly firm. With a hand mixture or stand mixer, whip the butter mixture until light and fluffy for about 3 to 5 minutes. Add to mason jars and place back in the fridge to harden.

COMPOUND BUTTERS

These are fun ways to spice up the butter recipe on page 40, depending on what you're using the butter for. These three variations of the butter recipe are the ones that my grandmother used to make all the time with conventional butter. My favorite ways to use them are to add a small amount to the top of a filet mignon (see the Vegan Meats chapter) or spread them on bread instead of plain butter. That said, use them however you want—try them when making a grilled cheese to kick it up a notch. Flavored butters are a fun way to explore different flavor combinations and get creative!

METHOD:

1. Add the desired flavorings to one batch of room temperature butter (recipe on page 40), along with the salt and mix until well combined.

2. Place back into butter molds or roll into a log inside of some parchment paper or plastic wrap and place in the fridge for at least an hour to harden.

Yield: 2 cups (450 g) butter

Time: 1 hour

INGREDIENTS:

BASE

2 cups (450 g) vegan butter (see page 40 for recipe), at room temperature

½ teaspoon salt

CALABRIAN CHILE

¼ cup (112 g) finely chopped Calabrian chiles (or more)

GARLIC HERB

6 garlic cloves, minced

1 tablespoon each finely chopped fresh (3 g) basil, (4 g) parsley, (2 g) thyme, and (2 g) rosemary

WHITE TRUFFLE AND SAGE

2 teaspoons white truffle powder

1 tablespoon (3 g) finely chopped fresh sage

> **NOTE:**
>
> *These butters are great for cheese boards, on bread, to cook any of the vegan meats in this book in, or to use in place of normal butter in any recipe to add extra flavor!*

ROASTED GARLIC

Everyone should know how to make roasted garlic. It's a straightforward process, and as an ingredient, it seems to please those palates that don't care for raw garlic. That's because after roasting, you're left with a sweet, jam-like version of garlic that's much more mellow. It's a great way to add a subtle garlic flavor to any dish and can help balance out strong flavors in certain recipes, as in acidic white wine sauces or a rich, creamy Alfredo.

METHOD:

1. Preheat the oven to 425°F (220°C, or gas mark 7).

2. Take each head of garlic and, holding it sideways on the cutting board, cut off the top of the bulb that is starting to grow upward to reveal the garlic cloves. I recommend cutting about one-quarter of the way down the head of garlic from the top. Discard the tops or freeze them for making homemade vegetable broth.

3. Place each garlic head on a piece of aluminum foil that's large enough to wrap it up after seasoning.

4. Top each head with the olive oil, salt, and pepper. Wrap each bulb individually with foil and make sure they're all tightly wrapped and sealed before baking.

5. Place the aluminum foil packets on a baking tray and bake for 1 hour. Check after 45 minutes. They're ready when they're a deep golden brown. If they need to cook longer, continue to cook and check at 5-minute increments.

Yield: 6 heads of roasted garlic

Time: 1 hour 15 minutes

INGREDIENTS:

6 heads garlic

6 tablespoons (90 ml) olive oil (1 tablespoon [15 ml] per head of garlic)

3 teaspoons (18 g) salt (½ teaspoon per head of garlic)

3 teaspoons (6 g) black pepper (½ teaspoon per head of garlic)

Chapter 2

Vegan Cheeses

FRESH MOZZARELLA

Vegan fresh mozzarella isn't readily available in stores, and for Italian cooking, it's super important to have. It's a fun and easy cheese to make, as you can learn basic fermentation techniques. It slices well, melts great, browns with the best of them, and can be eaten both raw and cooked. It tastes amazing either way!

Yield: 6 to 12 mozzarella balls (depending on size)

Time: Cultured Cashew Milk 24 hours; Cheese 8 to 24 hours

METHOD:

1. To make the cashew milk: Drain and rinse the cashews. Blend the cashews, water, soy lecithin, and acidophilus powder together in a high-powered blender until well emulsified.

2. Transfer to an extremely clean (preferably freshly boiled) glass container. Cover with plastic wrap and set on the countertop for 12 to 24 hours. The longer it sits, the "tangier" the flavor will be.

3. To make the mozzarella: Add the cultured cashew milk, kappa carrageenan, lactic acid, tapioca starch, and salt to the high-powered blender. Blend until smooth.

4. Add the coconut oil and blend just until glossy and combined well.

5. Transfer the mixture to a saucepot over medium heat, whisking for about 30 seconds to a minute until the cheese starts to "break." Use an immersion blender to re-emulsify the cheese and continue to whisk consistently for another 2 to 3 minutes until thick.

6. Now, shape the mozzarella. This needs to be done quickly. To make a standard size mozzarella ball, use a 2-ounce (60 ml) disher and scoop two small balls from the mixture into the center of a piece of plastic wrap. Fold the plastic wrap over itself, grab the ends, and twist it around in a quick swinging motion until a larger ball forms. Tightly pull the two ends of plastic wrap under the ball and tie in a double knot.

7. Immediately place the wrapped mozzarella balls into an ice bath. Repeat using all of the mozzarella mixture. Transfer the ice bath to the fridge and allow to cool for about 8 hours.

8. Make the brine by slightly heating the water and stirring in the salt to dissolve. It should taste like lightly salty sea water. Let the brine cool.

9. After the ice bath, remove the cheese from the plastic wrap and add to the salt brine for 24 hours before consuming.

INGREDIENTS:

CULTURED CASHEW MILK

1 cup (140 g) raw unsalted cashews, soaked

4 cups (946 ml) water

2 tablespoons (15 g) soy lecithin

1 tablespoon (12 g) acidophilus powder (probiotic powder)

FRESH MOZZARELLA

5 cups (1.2 L) cultured cashew milk (1 recipe)

3 tablespoons (33 g) kappa carrageenan

1 teaspoon lactic acid

1 cup (120 g) plus 2 tablespoons (15 g) tapioca starch

1½ teaspoons salt

1½ cups (355 ml) melted (liquid) coconut oil

1 tablespoon (18 g) salt per 1 gallon (3.8 L) of water (brine)

NOTES:

- You can make any size mozzarella balls—super tiny ones or ones even bigger than the 4-ounce (115 g) ones shown here.

- The amount of time you allow the cashew milk to culture will give it a stronger flavor. For a very mild cheese, skip the culturing process altogether. Just follow the same steps but don't add the acidophilus powder and once you make the cashew milk, you can immediately continue making the cheese.

- Most of the miscellaneous ingredients like lactic acid, kappa carrageenan, and acidophilus powder (probiotics available in powdered or capsule form) can be found online if you don't find them in a specialty store!

PARMESAN

Shave it, shred it, grate it, or melt it into a sauce. You can use it virtually any way you would use traditional Parmesan, and it's just as good. Heck, it's even better than your grandma's Parmesan. I always have some of this on hand because it's good on literally everything, and it's a staple in Italian cooking (but hey, you probably knew that already if you're reading this book!). With this specific recipe, you'll know you've nailed it if it forms into a fully solid wedge— it shouldn't fall apart when you pick it up and it should be a firm, stable block of cheese. Don't get it confused with mozzarella, which is very soft and stretchy.

Yield: 1 block of cheese (about 1 cup [120 g] grated)

Time: 15 minutes

INGREDIENTS:

1¾ cups (382 g) unrefined coconut oil, melted

1¼ cups (295 ml) filtered water

2 teaspoons (10 ml) extra-virgin olive oil

4 teaspoons (24 g) sea salt

2 tablespoons (29 g) soy lecithin

1½ cups (288 g) potato starch

1 cup (158 g) rice flour

¼ cup (25 g) brown rice protein powder

2½ tablespoons (20 g) nutritional yeast

METHOD:

1. Place the melted coconut oil, water, extra-virgin olive oil, salt, and soy lecithin in a blender. Blend on high for about 2 minutes, making sure the oil and water are well emulsified.

2. Place the rest of your ingredients in a pot and add the oil and water mixture as well. Heat over medium-low heat, whisking constantly and quickly, for about 2 minutes, until the mixture becomes glossy.

3. Pour into a cake tin (or a few depending on the size you have) or cheese mold, tap a few times to remove any air bubbles, and immediately place in the fridge. I used a 10-inch (25 cm) round cake pan, which is ideal!

4. Allow to set overnight, then turn out of the mold and cut into wedges! You can slice it, shred it, or grate it, but make sure to keep it in the fridge right up until you add it to a dish or it will get soft.

NOTES:

• *If you want a grated Parmesan like the stuff you buy in a shaker bottle, take a chunk of the Parmesan and pulse lightly in a food processor until it resembles that same texture. You can even keep this in a shaker bottle in the fridge.*

• *You can grate this over a microplane, shred it, make ribbons using a peeler, or cut it into small cubes or slices for a cheese board.*

SHREDDED MOZZARELLA

Shredded mozzarella has its place in this book because it serves a different purpose than the fresh mozzarella. This mozzarella recipe yields a drier and firmer product than its fresh counterpart, so it's great for slicing thinly for sandwiches, shredding to top baked pasta dishes, or mixing into a pasta filling. You can flavor it however you want, making this incredibly versatile and customizable to your specific tastes.

Yield: About 4 cups (448 g) shredded

Time: 3 hours

INGREDIENTS:

1½ cups (355 ml) water

½ cup (70 g) raw unsalted cashews, soaked

4 tablespoons (30 g) tapioca starch

1 tablespoon (15 ml) white vinegar

1 tablespoon (15 ml) lemon juice

4 tablespoons (56 g) refined coconut oil

1½ teaspoons salt

1½ tablespoons (6 g) nutritional yeast

1½ tablespoons (17 g) kappa carrageenan

METHOD:

1. Boil the water.

2. Drain and rinse the cashews.

3. In a high-powered blender (like a Vitamix), add the cashews, tapioca starch, vinegar, lemon juice, coconut oil, salt, nutritional yeast, and kappa carrageenan. Blend together.

4. Slowly pour in the boiling water and instantly blend everything together. Use a kitchen towel over the lid to prevent burns! Blend this mixture until it's *completely* smooth! Scrape down the sides if necessary.

5. Pour the cheese mix into the desired molds. This mix sets quickly, so make sure to work fast!

6. Move the mold(s) to the fridge and allow to set for about 3 to 4 hours until completely solid.

7. After it has set, remove it from the mold, wrap in a paper towel, place in a zip-top bag or airtight container, and then back into the fridge!

8. It is now ready to be shredded or sliced whenever needed.

GOAT CHEESE

Goat cheese is like if feta and cream cheese had a baby. It has the tang of feta cheese but the texture of cream cheese. This recipe is awesome because you can crumble it and use it cold on top of salads or pizzas and you can bake it, brown it, or melt it down in any sauce. It's great for adding tang and brightness to your dish, whatever it may be.

Yield: About 2 cups (448 g), enough for 4 logs about 4 to 6 inches (10 to 15 cm) long

Time: 2 hours

METHOD:

1. Add all the ingredients to a food processor and pulse to combine into a paste.

2. Take a piece of plastic wrap and scoop some of the mixture into the center; about ½ cup (112 g) or ¾ cup (168 g) will do, depending on how big you want your goat cheese log. Roll up tightly into a sausage or log shape.

3. Place in the fridge for at least 6 hours to set, though overnight is best.

INGREDIENTS:

1 block extra-firm tofu

1 tablespoon (16 g) white miso paste

¼ cup (60 ml) melted coconut oil

¼ cup (60 ml) rice vinegar

1 teaspoon sea salt

NOTES:

• *Once the goat cheese is set, you can crumble it, slice it, and add it to pastas, pizzas, and more.*

• *You can also add dried or fresh herbs, nuts, or dried fruit of your choosing by rolling your goat cheese logs in them for charcuterie boards!*

RICOTTA

Everyone knows the classic ricotta! It's heavily used in both traditional Italian and Italian American dishes, and it can be used in both sweet and savory recipes. You use it to fill cannoli just as easily as ravioli. The opportunities are endless, and it's a staple recipe that every home chef should know when they embark on their plant-based journey into Italian cooking.

Yield: About 4 cups (1 kg)

Time: 5 minutes

INGREDIENTS:

1 block (16 ounces, or 455 g) medium firm tofu

1½ teaspoons garlic powder

1½ teaspoons salt

2 teaspoons nutritional yeast

1½ teaspoons white vinegar

1 tablespoon (15 ml) olive oil

1 tablespoon (15 ml) plain unsweetened soy milk

METHOD:

1. Place all of the ingredients except the milk in a food processor.

2. Pulse a few times until the tofu has a bit of crumb to it.

3. Slowly add the milk while pulsing. The ricotta can either be left with a bit of "curd" or processed until it's completely smooth.

4. Taste and adjust the salt if needed and place in a covered container in the fridge for up to a week.

BURRATA

You may not have heard of burrata, but it's a super versatile cheese you can use in salads, on top of pasta, in sauces, or you can just eat it totally on its own. It's good pretty much no matter how you eat it! You know you've done it right when you cut the ball in half and the creamy goodness of the curds in the center oozes out, which might sound strange, but I promise you, it's going to be one of your favorites after you make it for yourself. This is a cheese that just recently became more popular, and I'm so excited to have a vegan version of it you can make for yourself. It's worth the effort; trust me.

Yield: 6 to 8 burrata balls

Time: 30 minutes

INGREDIENTS:

½ cup (70 g) raw unsalted cashews, soaked

2 cups (475 ml) water

1 tablespoon (8 g) soy lecithin

1 tablespoon (12 g) acidophilus powder (probiotic)

1 teaspoon salt

½ block (8 ounces, or 225 g) firm tofu, crumbled

Fresh Mozzarella from page 48

METHOD:

1. Drain and rinse the cashews.

2. To make the curd mixture for the center, blend the cashews, water, soy lecithin, and acidophilus powder and culture it on the counter for 24 hours. This is the same process as the fresh mozzarella, just a half batch of the liquid! A full batch of this has to be made anyway for the outside of the burrata, so it can be cultured all together.

3. Once cultured, take one-quarter of a block of tofu and blend it with half the amount of cultured cashew milk and salt in a food processor until it is the consistency of heavy cream. Then, add the other one-quarter of the tofu and pulse lightly until there are crumbled bits throughout, like cottage cheese.

4. Make the Fresh Mozzarella according to the recipe on page 48. When forming the mozzarella balls, place a dollop of mozzarella on the plastic wrap, place a spoonful of the curd mixture in the center, and top with a little more mozzarella. Form into balls the same way as the Fresh Mozzarella recipe and then place in the ice bath.

5. Finish the rest of the mozzarella recipe as stated. When the burrata ball is sliced open, the curd mixture will ooze out beautifully!

MASCARPONE

Mascarpone is an Italian cheese that is similar to ricotta or cream cheese, but it's sweet! It's mainly used in desserts and in savory dishes with intense flavors as it helps to balance those flavors out. It's perfect for tiramisu, cheesecakes, cookies, or even just as a dip for fruit.

Yield: About 2 cups (480 g)

Time: 10 minutes

METHOD:

1. Drain and rinse the cashews and almonds.

2. Put everything into a food processor and pulse until completely smooth.

3. Use as a 1:1 ratio in any recipe using mascarpone or use it as a delicious dip for fruit!

INGREDIENTS:

1¼ cups (175 g) raw unsalted cashews, soaked

¼ cup (28 g) slivered unsalted almonds, soaked

½ cup (115 g) plain vegan yogurt

1 tablespoon (15 ml) plus 2 teaspoons lemon juice

3 teaspoons (15 ml) white vinegar

¼ teaspoon salt

2½ teaspoons (10 g) organic cane sugar

NOTES:

• *If you want a lighter and fluffier end result, use ½ cup (55 g) almonds . . . but if you want it thicker and heavier, use all cashews!*

• *Make sure to use slivered unsalted almonds. These are important because the skin is already removed, and the skin can change the color and texture of the cheese.*

• *A higher fat content, creamier yogurt will work best. A thick coconut or cashew yogurt is ideal!*

• *You can leave the sugar out if you want something that's just pure tang, but then that basically makes this a very smooth ricotta!*

Chapter 3

Vegan Meats

GROUND BEEF

This ground beef recipe is one of the most versatile in this book. You can sauté it, turn it into meatballs, and even make burgers with it (not very Italian, I know). It's great in soups and stews as well. This is your vegan go-to for replacing ground beef in any non-vegan recipe.

Yield: 1½ pounds (680 g)

Time: 20 minutes

INGREDIENTS:

1 cup (235 ml) vegetable broth

2 tablespoons (32 g) tomato paste

2 tablespoons (28 ml) soy sauce

1 tablespoon (15 ml) vegan Worcestershire sauce

2 teaspoons garlic powder

2 teaspoons onion powder

½ teaspoon paprika

½ teaspoon sea salt

¼ teaspoon white pepper

¼ teaspoon beet powder

1 cup (100 g) TVP (textured vegetable protein)

3 tablespoons (45 ml) melted refined coconut oil

2½ teaspoons (10 g) potato starch

METHOD:

1. In a saucepot on the stovetop, heat up the vegetable broth, tomato paste, soy sauce, Worcestershire sauce, garlic powder, onion powder, paprika, salt, white pepper, and beet powder to a light simmer.

2. Pour over the top of the TVP in a bowl and cover with plastic wrap or a plate. Let sit for 5 to 10 minutes until the TVP has absorbed all of the liquid. Mix in the melted coconut oil and potato starch by hand (be careful it's not too hot!) until everything is well combined.

3. Use like normal ground beef in any recipe.

CHICKEN CUTLETS

Want to make chicken Parmesan, chicken Milanese, grill chicken breast to top a Caesar salad, or shred chicken to fill a ravioli? This is the perfect base for any of these dishes and beyond. You can form this vegan chicken into whatever shape you want, making it versatile in a variety of different recipes.

Yield: about 10 cutlets

Time: 1 hour 45 minutes

INGREDIENTS:

CHICKEN

1 block (15.5 ounces, or 435 g) soft tofu, drained

1 can (16 ounces, or 448 g) Great Northern beans, including the liquid in the can

6 tablespoons (90 ml) canola oil, divided

Sea salt to taste

2½ tablespoons (40 g) white miso paste

1 tablespoon (15 ml) white wine vinegar

2 teaspoons garlic powder

2 teaspoons onion powder

1 teaspoon poultry seasoning

3½ cups (385 g) vital wheat gluten

METHOD:

1. To make the cutlets: Add all of your chicken ingredients, besides the vital wheat gluten, to a high-powered blender and blend until completely smooth.

2. Transfer the mixture to a bowl and add the vital wheat gluten. Knead for 15 to 20 minutes until a firm ball forms.

3. Divide the dough into approximately 10 pieces or make them smaller or bigger depending on what the cutlets are being used for. Working with one piece at a time, pinch the edges of the mixture, also called seitan, and tuck it over to the center, making one smooth side and one folded side—like a roll. Flatten each piece of dough to about ½ inch (1 cm) thick and shape to your preference.

4. Lay a sheet of parchment paper out and place a cutlet on top. Fold all the sides over and wrap very tightly. Repeat with all pieces. Make sure they are wrapped *very* tightly to not let the seitan expand too much. Follow the same process with a couple layers of plastic wrap outside of the parchment paper, again wrapping tightly.

Continued >

5. Place the wrapped chicken cutlets into a steamer and steam for at least 1 hour and 45 minutes, or up to 2 hours. Once steamed, remove the seitan from the steamer and allow to cool for 20 minutes still wrapped.

6. For the brine: Add all of the brine ingredients to a large mixing bowl and whisk until everything is well combined.

7. Once the seitan cutlets are cooled, unwrap them and add them to the bowl of brine. Cover and place in the fridge overnight.

8. The next day, the cutlets will be ready to use like a normal piece of chicken!

BRINE

6 garlic cloves, crushed

1 cup (235 ml) Pinot Grigio

2½ cups (588 ml) hot water

2 tablespoons (18 g) vegan chicken bouillon

Sea salt to taste, plus a bit extra (you want it to be *just* too salty)

6 bay leaves

4 sprigs fresh tarragon

NOTE:

Some of my favorite ways to use these chicken cutlets are in Chicken Parmesan (page 200), Chicken Milanese (page 203), Caesar Salad (page 180), and as the filling for Ricotta and Chicken Mezzalune (page 143).

BACON AND PANCETTA

Bacon and pancetta are two sides of the same coin—bacon is essentially the smoked, American version of pancetta. Making these dishes vegan are identical processes, save for the addition of liquid smoke to make the pancetta into bacon. Pancetta is primarily used in Italian dishes in place of bacon, but bacon still has its place, especially in Italian American cuisine. This recipe is a favorite of mine because you get that fatty streakiness that bacon and pancetta have. You can cut it into strips, dice it into cubes, bake it, or do whatever you would normally do with non-vegan bacon or pancetta.

METHOD:

1. To make the red parts: In a blender, add the wet ingredients for both parts separately and blend until completely smooth. Set aside in jars or bowls.

2. In two large bowls, add the dry ingredients for the red part in one and the white part in the other. Whisk well to combined.

3. Pour the designated wet mix over each of its dry mixture and mix each of them very well. I recommend doing these one at a time.

4. The dough will form a relatively firm ball. Once this happens, place it on a clean floured surface. Knead the mixture for 15 to 17 minutes. After kneading, wrap the dough in plastic wrap and set aside to rest. Since it is a smaller amount, the white mixture only has to be kneaded for 10 to 12 minutes.

5. Take the red dough and roll it out into a rectangle about ¼ inch (6 mm) thick.

6. Take the white dough and roll it out into the same size rectangle, but about half the thickness of the red dough.

7. Lay the white dough on top of the red dough and press firmly together until they have become one piece of dough—without the colors mixing. Cut this in half and stack on top of each other, alternating red-white-red-white. Press this taller piece of dough together very firmly until it is one piece of dough—again, without the colors mixing.

Yield: 20 thick slices of bacon

Time: 3 hours

INGREDIENTS:

RED PART

Wet

1¼ cups (295 ml) vegetable broth

1 cup (235 ml) apple cider

¾ cup (53 g) dried porcini mushrooms

3 tablespoons (45 ml) soy sauce

6 tablespoons (90 ml) maple syrup

1½ tablespoons (24 g) white miso paste

4½ tablespoons (32 g) paprika

2¼ tablespoons (32 ml) hickory liquid smoke

1 large red onion, quartered (sautéed lightly in olive or grapeseed oil)

5 garlic cloves (sautéed lightly in olive or grapeseed oil)

½ cup (120 g) Great Northern/white beans

2½ teaspoons ground sage

1 teaspoon ground fennel

Sea salt to taste

Black pepper to taste

½ teaspoon beet powder

Continued >

8. Preheat a large saucepan of water over medium heat to a simmer. Then, wrap the dough tightly first in parchment paper, then plastic wrap. Make sure it is *very* tightly wrapped and sealed.

9. Place the tightly wrapped dough in the water and cook for 3 hours, flipping halfway through.

10. After 3 hours, remove it from the water. Once slightly cooled, unwrap the bacon and place it in the fridge overnight to cool completely, covered lightly with parchment paper.

11. Once cooled, slice to the desired thickness or dice and cook however regular bacon is used!

Dry

2¼ cups (270 g) vital wheat gluten

4 tablespoons (30 g) chickpea flour

4 tablespoons (16 g) nutritional yeast

WHITE PART

Wet

½ cup (126 g) medium firm tofu

½ cup (120 ml) plain unsweetened plant milk

½ cup (130 g) Great Northern/white beans

1¼ teaspoons onion powder

½ teaspoon garlic powder

1¼ tablespoons (20 g) white miso paste

Dry

1¼ cups (150 g) vital wheat gluten

3 tablespoons (23 g) chickpea flour

NOTES:

• *To make pancetta, follow the same instructions but leave out the liquid smoke (pancetta isn't smoked like American bacon is) and form it into a circle instead of a rectangle.*

• *I recommend kneading this dough with your hands. A lot of people use stand mixers, but that can easily overmix the dough and make it too tough.*

SHREDDED "BEEF" SHORT RIBS

Short rib ragu is something my family used to make all the time when I was a kid, and while it's very similar to Bolognese, it adds another level of texture that a Bolognese wouldn't have. You can use these short ribs in plenty of different recipes, but you'll want to start with a ragu. You can thank me later.

Yield: 1½ pounds (680 g)

Time: 1 hour

INGREDIENTS:

3 cups (700 ml) vegetable broth

½ cup (120 ml) soy sauce

¼ cup (60 ml) vegan Worcestershire sauce

2 tablespoons (30 g) smooth Dijon mustard

2 tablespoons (28 ml) rice vinegar

Salt and black pepper to taste

2 teaspoons garlic powder

2 teaspoons onion powder

2 cans (14 ounces, or 390 g each) brined jackfruit, rinsed and drained

METHOD:

1. In a saucepot over medium heat, add all of the ingredients except the jackfruit and whisk until well combined.

2. Rinse, drain, and remove the seeds from the jackfruit triangles. Add to the pot with the broth mixture and bring to a boil.

3. Once at a boil, decrease to a simmer and cook for 20 to 30 minutes until the broth has reduced by half.

4. Remove the jackfruit from the broth, shred it with two forks, and place back into the broth. Continue to cook for another 15 minutes until almost all of the liquid has evaporated. Use in any recipe that calls for shredded beef or short ribs!

HOT AND SWEET
ITALIAN SAUSAGE LINKS

Like the bacon and pancetta recipe (page 69), you're getting a two-in-one here. For sweet sausage links, leave out the crushed red pepper and for hot sausage links, add them! Adjust to your desired level of spice. This fun seitan recipe is easy to make for even the greenest of home chefs. You can grill these bad boys up whole, slice them and sauté them, or crumble them up into a ground sausage. They're packed full of flavor and are a spectacular addition to any Italian dinner table.

Yield: 6 to 8 sausage links

Time: 1 hour 20 minutes

INGREDIENTS:

2 tablespoons (28 ml) oil from the sun-dried tomato jar

1 medium yellow onion, chopped

5 garlic cloves, minced

¾ cup (355 ml) vegetable broth, warmed

¼ cup (65 g) tomato paste

¼ cup (63 g) white miso paste

¼ cup (28 g) sun-dried tomatoes in oil, finely chopped

2 tablespoons (8 g) nutritional yeast

1 tablespoon (2 g) dried basil

2 teaspoons brown sugar

2 teaspoons fennel seeds

1 teaspoon dried oregano

1 teaspoon finely chopped fresh rosemary

1 teaspoon finely chopped fresh thyme

1 teaspoon sea salt

1 teaspoon crushed red pepper (for the hot sausage links)

¼ teaspoon liquid smoke

2 cups (240 g) vital wheat gluten

METHOD:

1. In a skillet over medium heat, warm the oil from the sun-dried tomato jar until shimmering, then add the chopped onion and garlic. Cook for 5 to 7 minutes until slightly caramelized. Take off the stove and allow to cool to room temperature.

2. In a mixing bowl, add the warm vegetable broth, tomato paste, and miso paste and mix until combined and smooth.

3. Add the sun-dried tomatoes, nutritional yeast, herbs, sugar, spices, and liquid smoke. Mix well.

4. Add the vital wheat gluten and mix with a rubber spatula until a rough dough forms. Knead for about 5 minutes until the dough comes together.

5. Split your dough into 6 to 8 equal-size pieces. Place one piece on a sheet of aluminum foil (shiny side up), form into the shape of a sausage, and roll it up loosely, twisting the ends closed like a candy wrapper. Seal the ends firmly, but don't overtighten, as the sausages will expand as they cook. Repeat with all sausages.

6. Get a deep pot and add a steamer basket. Fill the pot with water until it's just under the steamer basket and bring to a boil. Add the sausages to the steamer basket and steam for 1 hour.

7. Remove the sausages from the steamer basket and let cool partially before transferring the foil-wrapped sausages to the refrigerator to cool completely overnight.

8. Once the sausages are cooled, remove the foil and slice, cook whole, or crumble.

MEATBALLS

In the United States, people associate meatballs with spaghetti. However, if you went to Italy and tried to order spaghetti and meatballs, you'd be sure to get a look of disapproval from the restaurant waitstaff. They're usually served as an entrée or in smaller portions as an appetizer alongside salad, nowhere near spaghetti. This vegan version is easy to make, and my Italian American self won't judge you if you eat them with spaghetti.

METHOD:

1. Mix the flax eggs in a bowl and allow to sit for 10 minutes to thicken.

2. Add all the ingredients except the oil to a large mixing bowl and mix well by hand to combine.

3. Roll the meatballs into slightly larger than golf ball–size balls and place on a plate until all are rolled.

4. Add the olive oil to a deep skillet over medium heat. Once it starts to shimmer, add the meatballs going around clockwise in the pan to keep track of which to flip first. After 3 to 4 minutes, starting with the first meatball put down and going around in order, flip them. The meatballs should be nice and browned on both sides.

5. Once they're browned, use them as is or transfer them into THE Tomato Sauce (see page 27 for recipe) to further cook and absorb that delicious sauce.

Yield: 12 to 15 meatballs (about 1½ pounds, or 680 g)

Time: 30 minutes

INGREDIENTS:

4 flax eggs (1 tablespoon ground [10 g] flax plus 2½ tablespoons [36 ml] water per egg)

1 pound (455 g) vegan ground beef (see page 64 for recipe)

2 teaspoons sea salt

1 tablespoon (10 g) minced garlic

½ cup (60 g) grated vegan Parmesan (see page 51 for recipe)

½ cup (60 g) Italian breadcrumbs

2 tablespoons (28 ml) olive oil

CHORIZO

Traditionally, chorizo is a type of Spanish or Mexican sausage (and yes, there's a difference between the two). However, Italian cooking utilizes chorizo in many creative and delicious ways. I know many vegan meats in this chapter are gluten-heavy, but carrots are surprisingly the tastiest way to make vegan chorizo. Providing you season them correctly, carrots transform during the cooking process to end up with something extremely like crumbled chorizo. You could say it's my own take on vegan "rabbit" food.

Yield: 1½ pounds (680 g)

Time: 20 minutes

INGREDIENTS:

1 pound 6 ounces (625 g) carrots, coarsely chopped

4 cups (946 ml) vegetable stock

2 tablespoons (28 ml) soy sauce

5 garlic cloves, minced

2 tablespoons (8 g) ancho chile powder

1 tablespoon (7 g) sweet paprika

1 teaspoon smoked paprika

1½ teaspoons salt

2 teaspoons dried oregano

½ teaspoon freshly ground black pepper

½ teaspoon ground cumin

½ teaspoon ground coriander

¼ teaspoon ground cinnamon

¼ teaspoon ground cloves

4 tablespoons (60 ml) apple cider vinegar

2 tablespoons (28 ml) red wine vinegar

3 tablespoons (45 ml) olive oil

METHOD:

1. In a food processor, add the coarsely chopped carrots and pulse a few times until it resembles chorizo crumbles.

2. In a stockpot, add the vegetable stock and soy sauce and bring to a low boil. Add the carrot crumbles and cook for about 1 to 2 minutes until slightly soft.

3. Drain the carrots (see note) and mix with the rest of the other ingredients except the olive oil.

4. Allow the carrots and spices to marinate ideally for 2 hours or overnight if desired!

5. When the carrot chorizo is ready, drain it, reserving the liquid. Add it along with the olive oil to a skillet over medium-high heat. Cook until it is golden brown and then pour in a little bit of the leftover marinade liquid (about 2 to 3 tablespoons [28 to 45 ml] worth) to steam the carrots and make them soft inside again.

6. Serve in any recipe that calls for crumbled chorizo.

> **NOTE:**
>
> *You can save the stock from step 3 for soups, stews, sauces, and more. Store it in the fridge for up to 2 days until ready to use.*

SCALLOPS

Scallops are popular in Italian dishes, but I have a confession to make—I never liked them, even before I went vegan. I wish I had known about a recipe like this because it gives such a similar texture and slight fishiness that scallops have without the slimy texture. I'm sure there are some of you that don't like mushrooms, but I promise you that you'll love this recipe. Even I love it, and I typically can't stand mushrooms of any kind! These are great for when you're making a special or romantic meal for a loved one.

Yield: 10 to 12 scallops

Time: 45 minutes

INGREDIENTS:

4 cups (946 ml) water

3 tablespoons (48 g) white miso

2 sheets nori

2 tablespoons (30 g) Dijon mustard

1 cup (235 ml) dry white wine

1 tablespoon (15 g) sea salt

2 teaspoons MSG (optional)

4 garlic cloves, crushed

2 tablespoons (28 ml) rice vinegar

4 to 6 large king oyster mushrooms

3 tablespoons (42 g) vegan butter (see page 40 for recipe)

METHOD:

1. In a stockpot over high heat, add the water, white miso, nori sheets, Dijon mustard, dry white wine, sea salt, MSG (if using), crushed garlic cloves, and rice vinegar. Bring to a boil and then reduce to a simmer.

2. Take the mushrooms and clean them with a damp paper towel. Cut the tops and bottoms off and cut into round "scallop" size pieces (about 1/2 to 3/4 inch [13 mm to 2 cm] thick).

3. Place the mushrooms in the simmering broth and reduce the heat to low. Allow to cook over low heat for 10 minutes. Then, remove from the heat, cover, and let rest for 30 minutes.

4. Remove the scallops from the broth and pat dry with a paper towel. Now, they're ready to use, the simplest way being sautéed in the butter with a touch of sea salt and pepper.

NOTES:

• *One fun way to cook these is to wrap them in some thinly sliced vegan bacon (see page 69 for recipe) before searing and cooking them in vegan butter (see page 40 for recipe), minced garlic, and a touch of dry white wine.*

• *Another delicious way to prepare these is serving them on top of some cooked orzo mixed with vegan butter (see page 40 for recipe) and freshly chopped parsley and topped with Sun-Dried Tomato Pesto (see page 167 for recipe).*

FILET MIGNON

Filet mignon is a delectable dish that many associate with dark, luxurious corners of upscale steakhouses. This recipe yields a similar texture and resemblance to that fatty, marbled filet everyone seeks. Once it's made, it can be cooked every way you can think of, and it's perfect for special occasions—especially if you're trying to impress guests.

METHOD:

1. Mix together the beef bouillon, cocoa powder, beet powder, marmite, mushroom powder, nutritional yeast, liquid smoke, salt, white pepper, and 2 tablespoons (28 ml) of water in a blender.

2. Once mixed, add the vital wheat gluten and pulse until the consistency is similar to ground meat. Remove from the blender and quickly get the next step done (this shouldn't rest as is for too long).

3. In a cup or bowl, combine the cornstarch, olive oil, and remaining water until smooth and then pour over the wheat gluten mixture.

4. Knead together by folding the meat onto itself in the same direction until firm.

5. Roll into a log about 3 to 4 inches (7.5 to 10 cm) wide. Wrap the filet in a sheet of parchment paper very tightly, twist the ends up, then wrap in a sheet of foil very tightly. Place in a steamer and steam for 1 hour.

6. Once the filet is done, remove from the steamer and let rest for 20 minutes wrapped. Then, unwrap and cut into two steaks.

    NOTE: *Save any ends and freeze them; after a while, you'll have enough to make a nice stew.*

7. The steaks are now ready to be seared, sautéed, or grilled to perfection.

Yield: 2 filets

Time: 1 hour 30 minutes

INGREDIENTS:

2 teaspoons vegan beef bouillon

2 teaspoons cocoa powder

1 tablespoon (10 g) beet powder

1 tablespoon (24 g) marmite

1 teaspoon mushroom powder

1 teaspoon nutritional yeast

2 drops liquid smoke

½ teaspoon sea salt

½ teaspoon white pepper

1 cup (235 ml) plus 2 tablespoons (28 ml) cold water, divided

1½ cups (180 g) vital wheat gluten

¼ cup (32 g) cornstarch

1 tablespoon (15 ml) olive oil

NOTE:

My favorite way to cook this: Heat 2 tablespoons (28 ml) of grapeseed oil in a pan over medium-high heat. Season generously with salt and black pepper and then sear the steaks on both sides until golden. Baste the steaks in 3 tablespoons (42 g) of vegan butter (see page 40), 3 crushed garlic cloves, and some fresh thyme and rosemary over medium heat for 3 to 4 minutes. Serve alongside mashed potatoes and roasted asparagus and top the steak with more butter from the pan.

Chapter 4

Baked Pastas

SAUSAGE AND RICOTTA STUFFED SHELLS WITH VODKA SAUCE

Traditionally, I would never pair vodka sauce with stuffed shells. However, I tried it on a whim and it completely changed my mind. Adding the sausage to the ricotta filling adds heartiness to the shells, and the vodka sauce adds extra depth and flavor that you'd miss out on otherwise.

Yield: 12 shells
(3 to 4 servings)

Time: 40 minutes

METHOD:

1. Preheat the oven to 400°F (200°C, or gas mark 6).

2. In a skillet over medium heat, add the olive oil and heat until shimmering, and then crumble in the sausage. Season with salt and pepper and cook for 5 to 7 minutes until browned. Set aside to cool for about 10 minutes.

3. In a large mixing bowl, add the ricotta, cooked sausage, parsley, basil, garlic powder, and salt and pepper to taste. Mix well until thoroughly combined.

4. Cook the shells in a large pot of boiling salted water until tender and then drain and rinse with cold water.

5. Fill the shells with the ricotta and sausage mixture.

6. In a baking pan, add 1½ cups (339 g) of sauce to the bottom of the pan and then place the shells on top. Spoon the remaining sauce over the shells, but don't cover them completely.

7. Either slice or shred the mozzarella and place some over each shell. Place in the preheated oven for 15 minutes and then switch to broil and broil for a few minutes until the cheese is bubbly and browned.

8. Top with more fresh basil if desired and serve!

INGREDIENTS:

2 tablespoons (28 ml) olive oil

1 pound (455 g) hot vegan Italian sausage (see page 75 for recipe)

Salt and black pepper to taste

2 cups (500 g) vegan ricotta (see page 56 for recipe)

4 tablespoons (16 g) chopped fresh parsley

4 tablespoons (10 g) chopped fresh basil, plus more for serving

1 tablespoon (9 g) garlic powder

1 box (1 pound, or 455 g) large shell pasta

2½ cups (565 g) vegan Vodka Sauce (see page 35 for recipe)

1 ball of fresh vegan mozzarella (see page 48 for recipe)

NOTE:

These stuffed shells are very versatile, filling-wise. You can do just ricotta, ricotta and sausage like in this recipe, or ricotta and spinach--or you can include more cheeses, veggies, or meats if you'd like! Just make sure your filling has a 2:1 ricotta cheese to other ingredients ratio.

LASAGNE BOLOGNESE

In the United States, people tend to think of lasagne as layers of wavy noodles and loads of ricotta cheese with ground beef, sauce, and so on. Traditionally, lasagne is made with several very thin layers of pasta and a bechamel sauce instead of ricotta. It's also typically made with a slow-cooked Bolognese instead of ground beef and you only put shredded cheese on the very top layer. It's definitely different than the American style, but I promise you it's better than any lasagne you've tried before. If you can master lasagne, it's the ultimate test of Italian cooking because of how many techniques are involved!

Yield: 9 servings

Time: 1½ hours

INGREDIENTS:

6 tablespoons (85 g) vegan butter (see page 40 for recipe)

6 tablespoons (48 g) all-purpose flour

3 cups (700 ml) plain unsweetened plant milk (preferably soy)

Salt and black pepper to taste

¼ cup (30 g) grated vegan Parmesan (see page 51 for recipe)

½ teaspoon freshly grated nutmeg

4 cups (1 kg) vegan Bolognese sauce (see page 28 for recipe)

10 vegan lasagne sheets (see page 19 for recipe)

1 ball of fresh vegan mozzarella (see page 48 for recipe)

Fresh basil

METHOD:

1. Preheat the oven to 375°F (180°C, or gas mark 4).

2. In a saucepot over medium heat, add the butter and heat until melted. Then, add the flour and whisk well. Cook while stirring constantly for 1 to 2 minutes until it's amber in color.

3. Add the milk 1 cup (235 ml) at a time, whisking well before adding more to fully incorporate the roux and get out any lumps.

4. Season with salt to taste and add the Parmesan and nutmeg. Stir well. Increase the heat to high and bring to a boil. Then, lower the heat to low and simmer, stirring frequently until the bechamel has thickened.

5. In a 9- × 13-inch (23 × 33 cm) baking dish (mine is about 3 to 4 inches [7.5 to 10 cm] deep), assemble in this order: Bolognese on the bottom to prevent sticking, lasagne sheets, more Bolognese, bechamel. Repeat the process until the baking dish is almost filled. For the final layer, top with the lasagne sheets and a tiny bit of bechamel.

6. Cover with foil and place into the preheated oven. Bake for 30 minutes.

7. Remove the foil, add the sliced fresh mozzarella on top, and bake for another 10 to 15 minutes. Then, broil for a few minutes until the cheese is bubbly and browned.

8. Let the lasagne cool for at least 20 minutes before cutting into it. Cut into slices and serve with extra sauce and topped with fresh basil.

Continued >

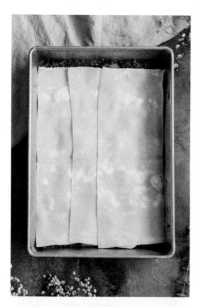

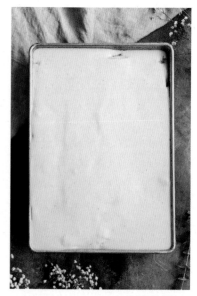

NOTES:

• *Alternate the direction you place the lasagne sheets every layer to ensure the dish stays together easier when serving.*

• *The best and neatest way to cut into this is to cook it the day before, cover, and place in the fridge overnight so everything sticks together. Then, reheat in the oven at 350°F (180°C, or gas mark 4) for an hour, covered. Even when slicing it hot, the time resting will help the slices hold together.*

• *If your pan is a different size or depth, just be flexible with the ingredient amounts called for here.*

BAKED RIGATONI

This is a dish that my family made for almost every holiday or special occasion you can think of. My aunt Debbie was the baked rigatoni queen (my grandmother refused to accept that anyone could outdo her). It's perfect for large parties because you can make a huge batch. It's creamy, it's hearty, it's cheesy—it's everything you could ask for when it comes to classic Italian American cooking.

Yield: 6 to 8 servings

Time: 25 minutes

INGREDIENTS:

1 pound (455 g) rigatoni

1 pound (455 g) vegan ground beef (see page 64 for recipe)

3 tablespoons (45 ml) olive oil

1 tablespoon (10 g) minced garlic

2 teaspoons dried oregano

Salt and black pepper to taste

2 cups (500 g) vegan ricotta (see page 56 for recipe)

3 cups (735 g) vegan tomato sauce, plus extra for serving (see page 27 for recipe)

1½ cups (168 g) shredded vegan mozzarella (see page 52 for recipe)

Grated vegan Parmesan (see page 51 for recipe)

Fresh basil

METHOD:

1. Cook the rigatoni in a large pot of boiling salted water until al dente.

2. In a skillet over medium heat, cook the ground beef in olive oil with the minced garlic, dried oregano, and salt and pepper until browned and cooked through. Allow to cool for a few minutes after cooking.

3. Drain the pasta and add it back to the pot. Add the ground beef and the oil included with it, the ricotta, and the tomato sauce.

4. Transfer to a baking dish and top with the shredded mozzarella. Place under the broiler until the cheese is melted and brown.

5. Top with Parmesan, fresh basil, and extra sauce if desired.

CAVATAPPI WITH VODKA SAUCE, KALE, AND GARLIC BREADCRUMBS

I created this recipe while experimenting with another pasta dish that I completely ruined! I had all these garlic breadcrumbs left over, and, wanting to make the most of what I had, I started pulling random ingredients I had in my kitchen. The final product ended up being such a hit that several friends requested I make it whenever they visit. I finally put the recipe in writing to share with the world. Sneaking the kale in adds a punch of nutritional value without compromising on flavor.

Yield: 8 to 10 servings

Time: 45 minutes

INGREDIENTS:

1 pound (455 g) cavatappi

2 to 3 cups (226 to 339 g) vegan Vodka Sauce (see page 35 for recipe)

1 bunch curly green kale, chopped with stems removed

1 packed cup (24 g) fresh basil, plus more for serving

1 cup (112 g) panko breadcrumbs

1 tablespoon (9 g) garlic powder

Salt and black pepper to taste

¼ cup (30 g) grated vegan Parmesan (see page 51 for recipe)

2 tablespoons (28 ml) melted vegan butter (see page 40 for recipe)

METHOD:

1. Preheat the oven to 400°F (200°C, or gas mark 6).

2. Cook the cavatappi in a large pot of boiling salted water until al dente. Drain with a slotted spoon into a mixing bowl and add a small amount of Vodka Sauce (mixed with the pasta) to prevent it from sticking.

3. In the leftover boiling water, blanch the chopped kale and whole fresh basil leaves for a minute or less until they're bright green, then transfer to an ice bath to stop the cooking.

4. Transfer the kale and basil to a fine-mesh sieve to drain excess water.

5. In a small mixing bowl, add the breadcrumbs, garlic powder, salt to taste, Parmesan, and melted butter. Mix well.

6. Add the kale and basil to the bowl with the pasta and add more sauce. Mix well until everything is combined. Add more sauce to the desired amount.

7. Transfer that mixture to a baking dish and top with the breadcrumb mixture. Place in the preheated oven, uncovered, for 15 to 20 minutes or until the breadcrumbs are golden brown.

8. Top with fresh basil when coming out of the oven and serve.

NOTES:

• *Add some shredded vegan mozzarella (see page 52 for recipe) underneath the breadcrumbs for an extra cheesy dish.*

• *You can broil the pasta dish to crisp up the breadcrumbs.*

PENNE ARRABBIATA PARMESAN

Think of this dish as the fired-up baked ziti you didn't know you needed. Using arrabbiata sauce gives it a kick and makes the dish satisfying, as it balances out the rich creaminess of the melted cheese on top of the pasta. It's quick to make and something you can prep in advance (if that's your style). Like baked ziti, it is generally a crowd-pleaser in large gatherings or family settings.

Yield: 6 to 8 servings

Time: 40 minutes

INGREDIENTS:

1 tablespoon (15 m) olive oil

1 medium yellow onion, diced

5 cloves garlic, minced

2 tablespoons (32 g) tomato paste

1 teaspoon to 1½ tablespoons crushed red pepper (to taste)

⅓ cup (80 ml) dry red wine

1 tablespoon (3 g) chopped fresh basil

2 tablespoons (8 g) chopped fresh parsley

1 tablespoon (15 ml) lemon juice

2 teaspoons dried oregano

Salt and black pepper to taste

2 cans (14 ounces, or 290 g) diced tomatoes and their juices

1 pound (455 g) penne

1 cup (112 g) shredded vegan mozzarella (see page 52 for recipe)

¼ cup (30 g) grated vegan Parmesan (see page 51 for recipe)

METHOD:

1. In a deep skillet over medium heat, add the olive oil along with the onion and garlic. Cook for 3 to 4 minutes until translucent and fragrant.

2. Stir in the tomato paste and crushed red pepper, stirring frequently, and cook for 1 to 2 minutes.

3. Add the red wine, basil, parsley, lemon juice, dried oregano, and black pepper. Bring to a boil and then reduce to a simmer for about 5 to 7 minutes.

4. Add the canned tomatoes, season to taste with salt and pepper, and stir well. Bring to a boil again and then reduce to a simmer and cook for 15 to 20 minutes.

5. Cook the penne in a large pot of boiling salted water until al dente and then drain.

6. Mix the cooked penne with the sauce and add to a baking dish.

7. Top with the shredded mozzarella and Parmesan and broil until the cheese is melted, browned, and bubbly.

BAKED MOZZARELLA GARLIC RIGATONI

If you love garlic, this is the dish for you. There are three different preparations of garlic present in this dish, all with their own flavor profile. The roasted garlic has a mellow, almost sweet taste; the fresh garlic hits you with pungent spice; and the powdered garlic gives you the nostalgic background taste of garlic that everyone knows and loves. The combination of the garlic flavors with the creamy cheese is what dreams are made of.

METHOD:

1. Preheat the oven to 400°F (200°C, or gas mark 6).

2. In a food processor, squeeze out all of the roasted garlic cloves and add the fresh garlic as well. Pulse until everything is very finely minced, almost to a paste.

3. Heat the Alfredo sauce in a saucepot and add the nutmeg, salt to taste, garlic powder, and the garlic mixture. Stir well to combine.

4. Cook the rigatoni in a large pot of boiling salted water until al dente and then drain. Mix the sauce and parsley (reserving a small amount for serving) in with the pasta.

5. Transfer to a baking dish and top with the shredded mozzarella.

6. Place in the oven and bake for 25 minutes and then broil for 1 to 2 minutes to get the cheese all bubbly and golden brown.

7. Remove from the oven, top with the remaining fresh parsley, and serve!

Yield: 6 to 8 servings

Time: 40 minutes

INGREDIENTS:

3 heads roasted garlic (see page 44 for recipe)

8 cloves fresh garlic

2 to 4 cups (452 to 904 g) vegan Alfredo sauce (see page 31 for recipe)

⅛ teaspoon freshly grated nutmeg

Salt to taste

2 teaspoons garlic powder

1 pound (455 g) rigatoni

¼ cup (15 g) chopped fresh parsley

1 cup (112 g) shredded vegan mozzarella (see page 52 for recipe)

CAVATELLI WITH SAUSAGE, TOMATOES, AND BROCCOLI RABE

Making this dish is a tale of two sauces—one being the white wine and Alfredo sauce and the second being the combination of goat cheese and burst cherry tomatoes. This all leads to a creamy and bright sauce that's insanely unique. Cavatelli noodles are the perfect vehicles for this type of sauce as well. Some people dislike broccoli rabe because of its bitter taste profile, but the sweetness from the tomatoes and the tanginess of the goat cheese mellow that out and make it delicious.

Yield: 6 to 8 servings

Time: 45 minutes

INGREDIENTS:

4 hot or sweet vegan Italian sausage links (see page 75 for recipe)

Olive oil, for sautéing

3 tablespoons (42 g) vegan butter (see page 40 for recipe)

4 garlic cloves, minced

2 cups (475 ml) dry white wine

¼ cup (35 g) raw unsalted cashews

½ to ¾ cup (120 to 175 ml) filtered water

1½ teaspoons Calabrian chiles

Salt and black pepper to taste

1 pound (455 g) cavatelli

1 pint (550 g) cherry tomatoes

1 bunch broccoli rabe, chopped into 1-inch (2.5 cm) pieces

1 cup (224 g) vegan goat cheese (see page 55 for recipe)

Lemon wedges

Fresh parsley

METHOD:

1. Preheat the oven to 350°F (180°C, or gas mark 4).

2. Slice the sausage into coins and cook in a skillet over medium heat with some olive oil until slightly browned. Set aside.

3. In the same pan, add the butter and minced garlic. Cook until fragrant and then add the white wine. Bring to a boil, reduce to a simmer, and cook for 3 to 4 minutes until slightly reduced.

4. In a high-powered blender, add the cashews, water, Calabrian chiles, and salt to taste. Blend until it is the consistency of heavy cream.

5. Add the Calabrian chile cashew cream to the white wine sauce, season with salt and pepper to taste, and cook until slightly thickened.

6. Cook the cavatelli in a large pot of boiling salted water until al dente and then drain. Add to a mixing bowl with the whole cherry tomatoes, chopped broccoli rabe, and the sauce. Mix well.

7. Transfer to a baking dish and cover with the goat cheese. Place in the preheated oven and bake for 25 to 30 minutes until the cherry tomatoes are ready to pop.

8. Once removed from the oven, stir everything together and burst all of the tomatoes. Serve with lemon wedges and top with fresh parsley!

ORECCHIETTE WITH PESTO CREAM AND WALNUT CRUMBLE

If you've never heard of orecchiette before, it means "little ear" in Italian. They're these little round noodles that have a bit of an edge to them, and they're typically not used in any sort of baked pasta dish. With this recipe, it's perfect because the little dip in the noodle picks up the walnut crumble in the sauce. It's great if you're looking to expand your palate beyond the realm of the typical Italian red sauces because it introduces bold flavors from the pesto and the walnut crumble.

Yield: 6 to 8 servings

Time: 30 minutes

INGREDIENTS:

2 cups (488 g) vegan Alfredo sauce (see page 31 for recipe)

⅓ cup (87 g) Basil Pesto (see page 167 for recipe)

1 pound (455 g) orecchiette

1 pint (550 g) cherry tomatoes, halved

¼ cup (25 g) walnuts

¼ cup (30 g) plain breadcrumbs

¼ cup (30 g) grated vegan Parmesan (see page 51 for recipe)

1 head roasted garlic (see page 44 for recipe)

Salt and black pepper to taste

Fresh basil

METHOD:

1. Preheat the oven to 500°F (250°C, or gas mark 10).

2. In a bowl, mix the Alfredo sauce and Basil Pesto together to create a pesto cream sauce.

3. Cook the orecchiette in a large pot of boiling salted water until al dente and then drain. Transfer to a mixing bowl.

4. Add the halved cherry tomatoes and sauce to the pasta and mix well to combine. Transfer to a baking dish.

5. For the walnut crumble, in a food processor, add the walnuts, breadcrumbs, Parmesan, roasted garlic cloves, and salt and pepper to taste and pulse until everything is around the same size as the breadcrumbs and feels like wet sand.

6. Sprinkle the walnut crumble on top of the pasta and place in the oven for 10 minutes or until the crumble has crisped up.

7. Remove from the oven and top with more Parmesan and fresh basil if desired.

Chapter 5

Fancy Pastas

CACIO E PEPE

Cacio e pepe is a classic Italian dish that's fast, easy, and filling. You can almost think of it like Italian mac and cheese (which doesn't really exist), and it's perfect after a long day when you're not feeling terribly fancy. Personally, I love making this when I get home after grabbing drinks with friends, since it doesn't require a ton of effort and hits the spot like you'd expect from a hearty Italian dish. That said, it's also simple enough to make with your kids when you're settling in for a cozy evening.

Yield: 4 servings

Time: 10 minutes

INGREDIENTS:

6 tablespoons (36 g) freshly cracked black pepper

1 pound (455 g) spaghetti

1 cup (120 g) grated vegan Parmesan (see page 51 for recipe)

½ cup (120 ml) reserved pasta water

METHOD:

1. In a skillet over medium heat, add the cracked black pepper to the dry pan. Toast for 1 minute, moving it around frequently.

2. Cook the spaghetti in a large pot of boiling salted water until almost al dente and then drain, reserving ½ cup (120 ml) of the pasta water.

3. Add the Parmesan, pasta, and reserved pasta water to the skillet with the pepper. Stir quickly over medium-low heat to emulsify the sauce and melt the cheese. Continue to cook until the pasta is al dente.

4. Plate and top with more freshly cracked black pepper and Parmesan.

PANCETTA AND PEA LINGUINE

This was a dish my grandmother cooked frequently because she always had leftover pancetta from making carbonara. She used to tell me that there's something magical about combining pancetta, peas, and lemon—and I have to agree! You'll find this is a quick dish you can easily scale to whip up for a group of people. (It was common for my grandmother to make it for fifteen to twenty people.) And they'll leave happy: it's a light dish despite what you might think because of the pancetta!

Yield: 4 servings

Time: 15 minutes

INGREDIENTS:

2 tablespoons (28 ml) olive oil

1 cup (147 g) vegan pancetta (see page 69 for recipe)

1 cup (235 ml) dry white wine

3 tablespoons (42 g) vegan butter (see page 40 for recipe)

½ cup (60 g) grated vegan Parmesan (see page 51 for recipe)

1 cup (130 g) frozen peas

Juice of half a lemon

1 teaspoon lemon zest

1 teaspoon salt

½ tablespoon black pepper

1 pound (455 g) linguine

¼ cup (60 ml) reserved pasta water

4 tablespoons (16 g) finely chopped fresh parsley

METHOD:

1. In a deep skillet over medium heat, add the olive oil and pancetta. Cook for 5 minutes until it starts to brown and crisp up.

2. Add the white wine, butter, Parmesan, peas, lemon juice and zest, salt, and pepper. Stir frequently to emulsify the sauce over medium heat.

3. Cook the linguine in a large pot of boiling salted water until almost al dente and then transfer with a slotted spoon directly into the saucepan along with ¼ cup (60 ml) of the pasta water.

4. Toss well to combine over low heat until the pasta is al dente.

5. Transfer to a large serving bowl or individual bowls and top with 1 tablespoon (4 g) of fresh parsley per serving and more Parmesan.

ROASTED FENNEL
AND SAUSAGE RIGATONI

Traditionally, Italian sausage has fennel seeds in it, which gives it its distinct flavor. With that in mind, adding roasted fennel to a pasta dish with sausage is a combination that makes so much sense. It amplifies the flavor of the sausage and makes everything that much more delicious. Also, let's talk for a minute about the delicious taste of roasted fennel. Cooking it in this way mellows out a lot of the harsher, licorice flavors into something sweeter. It's a unique flavor profile that I think will surprise you! Regardless of the type of sausage you use, it'll be a showstopper, but I recommend using the hot Italian sausage (page 75).

Yield: 4 servings

Time: 45 minutes

INGREDIENTS:

2 heads fennel

5 tablespoons (75 ml) olive oil, divided

2 teaspoons sea salt, divided

6 tablespoons (85 g) vegan butter (see page 40 for recipe), divided

1 large shallot, diced

1 head roasted garlic (see page 44 for recipe), chopped

½ teaspoon crushed red pepper

4 hot vegan Italian sausage links (see page 75 for recipe), sliced

2 teaspoons black pepper

2 cups (475 ml) dry white wine

1 pound (455 g) rigatoni

Juice of half a lemon

1 cup (235 ml) reserved pasta water

Grated vegan Parmesan (see page 51 for recipe)

Fennel fronds

METHOD:

1. Preheat the oven to 400°F (200°C, or gas mark 6).

2. Chop the fronds and long pieces off the fennel until it's just the bulb. Remove the first outer layer and cut off the root. Cut the fennel into bite-size cubes and place on a baking tray. Reserve the fennel fronds.

3. Drizzle the fennel with 3 tablespoons (45 ml) of olive oil and 1 teaspoon of sea salt. Toss well and bake for 25 to 30 minutes until tender.

4. In a deep skillet or saucepot over medium heat, add the remaining 2 tablespoons (28 ml) of olive oil and 3 tablespoons (42 g) of butter and heat until shimmering. Add the diced shallot, roasted garlic, and crushed red pepper. Cook for 2 to 3 minutes until fragrant and then add the sliced sausage.

5. Add the remaining 1 teaspoon of salt and the black pepper and cook until the sausage has browned. Remove the fennel from the oven and add to the pan as well.

6. Add the white wine and cook until reduced by half.

7. Cook the rigatoni in a large pot of boiling salted water and once the pasta is almost cooked, transfer with a slotted spoon directly into the sauce. Add the remaining 3 tablespoons (42 g) of butter, lemon juice, and 1 cup (235 ml) of the pasta water. Mix very well and cook over medium heat for another 3 to 4 minutes until the sauce has thickened.

8. Plate the pasta and top with Parmesan and the reserved fennel fronds.

SWEET PEA AND TARRAGON ALFREDO

Tarragon isn't commonplace, but it should be. It reminds me of basil in flavor, just a little sweeter. It goes well with peas, so adding them to an Alfredo sauce is an affordable and easy way to make use of ingredients you might have hiding away in your pantry. It's cheap and fast, but certainly doesn't taste like it.

Yield: 4 servings

Time: 20 minutes

INGREDIENTS:

1 cup (130 g) frozen peas

2 cups (488 g) vegan Alfredo sauce (see page 31 for recipe)

1 tablespoon (4 g) chopped fresh tarragon, plus more for serving

½ teaspoon crushed red pepper

1 pound (455 g) pasta (any desired shape)

½ cup (120 ml) reserved pasta water

Salt and black pepper to taste

¼ cup (25 g) walnuts, chopped

Grated vegan Parmesan (see page 51 for recipe)

METHOD:

1. In a boiling pot of salted water, cook the peas for just 1 to 2 minutes. With a slotted spoon, remove the peas from the water and add them to a blender with the Alfredo sauce, tarragon, and crushed red pepper. Blend until smooth.

2. Cook the pasta in a large pot of boiling salted water until al dente and then drain, reserving 1 cup (235 ml) of the pasta water.

3. In a large bowl, mix the sauce with the pasta and about ¼ to ½ cup of reserved pasta water. Add additional pasta water only if needed. (I almost never need more than ½ cup [120 ml].) Season with salt and black pepper to taste.

4. Serve family style in the large bowl, topped with chopped walnuts, Parmesan, and more fresh tarragon.

SWEET POTATO GNOCCHI WITH BROWN BUTTER AND SAGE

Gnocchi make for a rich, hearty dish that's perfect for the fall! Sweet potato and sage are the big flavors here, with the nuttiness of the browned butter bringing it all together. You can prepare the gnocchi ahead of time and freeze them to save time. This is one of my favorite dishes to make because of the flavor combinations and because when the gnocchi are already made, it's an easy meal as well.

Yield: 4 servings

Time: 10 minutes

INGREDIENTS:

½ cup (112 g) vegan butter (see page 40 for recipe)

¼ cup (10 g) fresh sage leaves, left whole

1 pound (455 g) sweet potato gnocchi (see page 22 for recipe)

¼ teaspoon salt

1 teaspoon black pepper

½ teaspoon crushed red pepper

1 tablespoon (15 ml) lemon juice

Grated vegan Parmesan (see page 51 for recipe)

METHOD:

1. Add the butter and sage leaves to a skillet over medium heat. Cook until the butter becomes an amber color and starts to smell nutty. It will also start to foam slightly. Immediately remove the brown butter from the heat and transfer to a bowl to stop it from cooking further. Set aside.

2. Cook the gnocchi for 1 to 2 minutes in a large pot of salted water just until they start to float.

3. Add the drained gnocchi to a large frying pan over medium heat along with the butter and sage. As the gnocchi start to sizzle, add the salt, black pepper, crushed red pepper, and lemon juice. Cook for a few minutes until the gnocchi crisp slightly.

4. Transfer everything to individual serving bowls and top with Parmesan.

SHORT RIB RAGU WITH PAPPARDELLE AND RICOTTA

This ragu is similar to a Bolognese, but on the next level. Using shredded beef instead of ground beef, mixed with white wine (instead of red), and with the addition of a handful of herbs, it's a combination you'll keep coming back to.

Yield: 4 to 6 servings

Time: 2 hours 30 minutes

METHOD:

1. In a large heavy-bottomed pot, add a few tablespoons (45 to 60 ml) of olive oil and brown the shredded short ribs. Remove and set aside.

2. In a food processor, add the carrots, celery, onion, and garlic. Run on high until everything is chopped *very* fine, almost into a "pulp."

3. Add the remaining ⅓ cup (80 ml) of olive oil to the same pan. Once the oil is shimmering, add the veggie mixture and salt and pepper to taste. Cook over medium heat for about 10 minutes until the vegetables have softened.

4. Add the tomato paste and cook for 2 to 3 minutes, stirring frequently.

5. Add the white wine and increase the heat to high. Bring to a boil and cook for 5 to 10 minutes until the liquid has reduced by half.

6. Use butcher's twine to tie the rosemary, thyme, and bay leaves into a bundle. Add that to the pan.

7. Add the crushed tomatoes, stir well, reduce to a simmer, and cover halfway with a lid. Cook for about 1 hour over low heat, stirring enough to prevent anything from sticking to the bottom of the pan.

8. After 1 hour, add the short ribs, butter, and Parmesan. Stir to combine. Cover halfway with a lid and cook for another hour, again stirring to prevent sticking.

9. Cook the pappardelle in a large pot of boiling salted water until almost al dente.

10. Transfer the pasta with a slotted spoon directly into a sauté pan along with a tiny bit of butter, Parmesan, and just enough sauce to fully coat the pasta. Add a tiny bit of the pasta water and stir over low heat for 2 minutes. Serve topped with ricotta and fresh basil.

INGREDIENTS:

⅓ cup (80 ml) plus a few tablespoons (45 to 60 ml) olive oil, divided

1 pound (455 g) shredded vegan short ribs (see page 72 for recipe)

3 medium-large carrots, peeled

3 ribs celery

1 large yellow onion

8 large garlic cloves

Salt and black pepper to taste

2 tablespoons (32 g) tomato paste

1 bottle (750 ml) Pinot Grigio

2 sprigs fresh rosemary

8 sprigs fresh thyme

3 bay leaves

1 can (28 ounces, or 785 g) crushed tomatoes

4 tablespoons (55 g) vegan butter (see page 40 for recipe), plus more for cooking

4 tablespoons (30 g) grated vegan Parmesan (see page 51 for recipe), plus more for cooking

1 pound (455 g) pappardelle (see page 19 for recipe)

Vegan ricotta (see page 56 for recipe)

Fresh basil

SUN-DRIED TOMATO PESTO GNOCCHI

Sun-dried tomato pesto deserves more attention that it gets—it adds an earthy, sweet flavor to a dish you'll never get from a traditional pesto. These gnocchi are one of the heavier pasta options since they're made with potatoes. (They're more like dumplings than pasta!) The pesto gives the gnocchi a brightness and lightness that lifts this up and keeps it from feeling like a heavy dish. If you have leftover pesto from another recipe, this is a perfect way to spruce it up.

Yield: 4 servings

Time: 15 minutes

INGREDIENTS:

1 tablespoon (14 g) vegan butter (see page 40 for recipe)

2 garlic cloves, thinly sliced

½ cup (130 g) Sun-Dried Tomato Pesto (see page 167 for recipe)

1 cup (235 ml) Pinot Grigio

1 pound (455 g) potato gnocchi (see page 22 for recipe)

Grated vegan Parmesan (see page 51 for recipe)

Fresh basil

METHOD:

1. In a saucepan over medium heat, add the butter and garlic and cook for a few minutes until the garlic is slightly golden.

2. Add the Sun-Dried Tomato Pesto and wine and raise the heat until the mixture comes to a boil. Once it hits a boil, immediately reduce to a simmer and cook for 5 to 10 minutes until the liquid has reduced by half. Turn off the heat and place a lid on the pot to keep warm while the gnocchi cooks.

3. Boil the gnocchi in a large pot of salted water until they float; then, cook 1 minute more.

4. Using a slotted spoon, transfer the gnocchi directly into the sauce along with a splash of hot pasta water to loosen and warm the sauce.

5. Transfer to individual serving bowls and top with Parmesan and fresh basil before serving.

KALE ALFREDO WITH CHORIZO AND FARFALLE

By now, you might be wondering why there are so many Alfredo recipes in this book. Alfredo is such a perfect base sauce, and it's delicious in almost every situation. This dish is great for sneaking veggies into a dinner even if you're not (or someone in the house is not) a huge fan of kale. (Also, the chorizo in this recipe is made from carrots!) While this isn't a recipe that I grew up eating, it's a perfect example of how to use the fundamentals of vegan cooking to experiment and create your own combinations of flavors—the best ones will become a staple of your own kitchen!

Yield: 4 servings

Time: 20 minutes

INGREDIENTS:

3 to 4 tablespoons (45 to 60 ml) olive oil

1 cup (118 g) vegan chorizo (see page 79 for recipe)

2 cups (134 g) lacinato kale, destemmed

2 cups (488 g) vegan Alfredo (see page 31 for recipe)

5 to 8 basil leaves, plus more for serving

1 pound (455 g) farfalle (see page 19 for recipe)

Crumbled vegan goat cheese (see page 55 for recipe)

METHOD:

1. In a large heavy-bottomed pot, add the olive oil and brown the chorizo. Set aside. Alternatively, the chorizo can be cooked the day before and reheated.

2. Bring a large pot of salted water to a boil. Once the water is boiling, add the kale and blanch for about 1 minute and then remove with a slotted spoon and add it to a blender.

3. Add the Alfredo and basil to the blender. Blend until smooth and set aside.

4. Cook the farfalle in the boiling water until almost al dente and then drain, reserving a bit of pasta water.

5. In a large pan, toss the pasta with the sauce and a little bit of pasta water.

6. Transfer to individual serving bowls and top with the cooked chorizo and crumbled goat cheese, along with more fresh basil, if desired.

CARBONARA

Before I went vegan, carbonara was my favorite pasta dish. Why? Because I was obsessed with eggs. There was a time when I made carbonara two to three times a week, every week. It took me a long time to make it vegan and have it taste just as good, so I'm excited to share this recipe. The creamy richness of the sauce mixed with salty pancetta and bright flavor of the peas is a magical combination bestowed upon us by the Italian cooking gods.

METHOD:

1. In a skillet over medium heat, add the olive oil, shallot, and garlic. Cook until fragrant, about a minute, and then add the pancetta and cook until golden. Turn off the heat and set aside.

2. In a boiling pot of salted water, cook the peas for just 1 to 2 minutes. With a slotted spoon, remove the peas from the water.

3. Cook the pasta in the same pot of boiling water until al dente and then drain, reserving 1 cup (235 ml) of the pasta water. Set the pasta and water aside.

4. For the "yolk" part of the sauce, blend the tomatoes, 4 tablespoons (60 ml) of melted butter, vegetable broth, plant milk, nutritional yeast, cornstarch, turmeric, garlic powder, black salt, and sea salt in a blender. Add this mixture to a pot over medium heat, whisking continuously while cooking for about 5 minutes. Once the liquid has thickened a bit, add the remaining 2 tablespoons (28 g) of butter and whisk until glossy. Set aside.

5. Over low heat, add the cooked pasta to the skillet with the pancetta. Add a little bit of pasta water and the Alfredo sauce. Stir well while adding the peas. Mix everything together well, adding a few dollops of the yolk sauce and more to taste if needed. Reserve some pancetta for the top.

6. Dish the pasta into individual serving bowls, dividing the extra ½ cup (74 g) of pancetta on top, along with some Parmesan, fresh parsley, and lots of pepper.

Yield: 4 servings

Time: 25 minutes

INGREDIENTS:

3 tablespoons (45 ml) olive oil

1 shallot, minced

1 garlic clove, minced

1½ cups (221 g) vegan pancetta, diced into small cubes (see page 69 for recipe)

2 cups (260 g) frozen peas

1 pound (455 g) bucatini or tagliatelle

1 cup (155 g) grape or cherry tomatoes

6 tablespoons (85 g) vegan butter, divided (see page 40 for recipe)

½ cup (120 ml) vegetable broth

¼ cup (60 ml) plain unsweetened plant milk

3½ tablespoons (39 g) nutritional yeast

1½ teaspoons cornstarch

½ teaspoon turmeric

¼ teaspoon garlic powder

¼ teaspoon black salt

Sea salt to taste

1 cup (235 ml) reserved pasta water

2 cups (488 g) vegan Alfredo sauce (see page 31 for recipe)

Grated vegan Parmesan (see page 51 for recipe)

Fresh parsley

Black pepper to taste

LINGUINE WITH WHITE CLAM SAUCE

Just like clam chowder, there's a white and red version of clam sauce. I'm on team white sauce for soup and sauce! This dish was common in my house growing up and is popular among the Italian restaurants in Buffalo, New York, as well. I was never a huge fan of clams, but the other flavors balance everything out and I was a fan of this dish. When cooking vegan, clams are easily replaced with jackfruit or hearts of palm, both of which offer a similar flavor and texture since they're both generally brined. Even if you aren't vegan yourself but still don't like clams very much, you'll want to try this one out!

Yield: 4 servings

Time: 20 minutes

INGREDIENTS:

1 pound (455 g) linguine (see page 19 for recipe)

¼ cup (60 ml) olive oil

¼ cup (55 g) vegan butter (see page 40 for recipe)

2 tablespoons (20 g) minced garlic

½ cup (50 g) finely diced onion

2 cups (475 ml) dry white wine

2 teaspoons vegan Worcestershire sauce

2 cans (14 ounces, or 390 g each) brined jackfruit

½ sheet nori

Juice of 1 lemon

¼ cup (15 g) finely chopped fresh parsley, plus more for serving

1 cup (235 ml) reserved pasta water

Salt to taste

Grated vegan Parmesan (see page 51 for recipe)

METHOD:

1. Cook the linguine in a large pot of boiling salted water just until al dente and then drain, reserving 1 cup (235 ml) of the pasta water.

2. Meanwhile, heat the olive oil and butter in large skillet over medium heat. Sauté the garlic and onion until softened, about 2 minutes.

3. Add the wine and Worcestershire sauce. Bring to a simmer and then lower the heat and cook on low for about 10 minutes.

4. Rinse, drain, and remove the seeds from the jackfruit triangles. Add the jackfruit to a food processor along with the nori sheet. Pulse until well mixed and the consistency is "minced" to look like chopped clams.

5. Add the cooked linguine, jackfruit, lemon juice, parsley, and reserved pasta water to the sauce. Add salt to taste. Simmer for about 5 more minutes until the sauce is mostly absorbed.

6. Divide into individual serving bowls, top with Parmesan and fresh parsley, and serve.

LINGUINE PUTTANESCA

Puttanesca is a popular sauce in Italy! Save for the anchovies, everything else in it is already vegan. I never liked anchovies to begin with, so I didn't have a problem taking them out—however, I wanted to preserve the deep, salty flavor that they bring to this dish. To make it vegan, I instead use soy sauce (not very Italian, but that's okay!). I think you'll find it creates a flavor profile that's almost identical to the original sauce. If you love olives and capers, this one is for you.

METHOD:

1. In a large skillet or pot over medium heat, heat the olive oil. Add the garlic and cook until fragrant, about a minute.

2. Add the soy sauce and cook for just a minute before adding the crushed tomatoes, olives, capers, salt and black pepper, sugar, lemon juice, and crushed red pepper. Bring to a boil and then reduce the heat and let simmer for about 15 minutes.

3. Meanwhile, bring a large pot of salted water to a boil. Add the linguine and cook until al dente and then drain the pasta.

4. Toss the pasta in the sauce. Transfer to individual serving bowls, sprinkle with fresh parsley and Parmesan, and serve.

Yield: 4 servings

Time: 30 minutes

INGREDIENTS:

¼ cup (60 ml) olive oil

4 garlic cloves, smashed

1 teaspoon soy sauce

1 can (28 ounces, or 785 g) whole tomatoes, crushed by hand

½ cup (85 g) black olives

¼ cup (36 g) capers

Sea salt and black pepper to taste

½ teaspoon organic cane sugar

Juice of half a lemon

½ teaspoon crushed red pepper

1 pound (455 g) linguine (see page 19 for recipe)

Chopped fresh parsley

Freshly grated vegan Parmesan (see page 51 for recipe)

20 CLOVE GARLIC PENNE

It's right there in the name, folks. This dish is like aglio e olio e pepperoncino, if you've ever had the pleasure of trying it. This recipe takes that classic to a new level by using twenty cloves of garlic to perfume the pasta with flavor. So if you love garlic, this one is for you. (If you don't, I'm not sure why you decided to pick up a book about Italian cooking, but we can let it slide for now!) This is a quick recipe for the days you're feeling a little lazy or had too much wine before dinner.

Yield: 4 servings

Time: 15 minutes

INGREDIENTS:

⅓ cup (80 ml) olive oil

20 garlic cloves, thinly sliced

1 to 2 teaspoons crushed red pepper (to taste)

1 pound (455 g) penne

¼ to ½ cup (60 to 120 ml) reserved pasta water

Salt to taste

¼ cup (15 g) chopped fresh parsley

Grated vegan Parmesan (see page 51 for recipe)

METHOD:

1. In a skillet over medium heat, add the olive oil, garlic, and crushed red pepper. Cook until just golden and then turn off the heat and set aside.

2. Cook the penne in a large pot of boiling salted water until al dente and then drain, reserving 1 cup (235 ml) of the pasta water.

3. Add the pasta to the pan with the oil and garlic mixture, along with a splash of the reserved pasta water. Stir and cook over low heat for 1 to 2 minutes. Add salt to taste. Add a small amount of pasta water if things get too thick and sticky.

4. Mix in the fresh parsley and immediately plate, topping with Parmesan.

CREAMY GARLIC RIGATONI

This one isn't too far removed from your traditional Alfredo. An insane amount of garlic and even more cheese turn it into an evolved form of the humble Alfredo. My grandmother would make this dish when she had a bunch of garlic that was about to go bad (a rare occurrence, but it happened). Whenever we had this, it was a special treat, and it still feels like a treat whenever I decide to make it. Using rigatoni, penne, or another hollow pasta instead of fettucine helps retain all that sauce and makes it so that every bite has a burst of flavor.

Yield: 4 servings

Time: 10 minutes

INGREDIENTS:

2 to 4 cups (488 to 976 g) Alfredo sauce (see page 31 for recipe)

⅛ teaspoon freshly grated nutmeg

Salt to taste

2 teaspoons garlic powder

8 cloves garlic, minced

1 pound (455 g) rigatoni

¼ cup (15 g) chopped fresh parsley

Grated vegan Parmesan (see page 51 for recipe)

METHOD:

1. Heat the Alfredo sauce in a saucepot and add the nutmeg, salt, garlic powder, and minced garlic. Stir well to combine.

2. Cook the rigatoni in a large pot of boiling salted water until al dente and then drain. Pour the sauce over the pasta and add the fresh parsley, reserving a small amount for garnish.

3. Top with the remaining parsley and Parmesan cheese, then serve.

Chapter 6

Filled Pastas

Pasta Essentials: Filled Pasta

Making filled pasta starts with making fresh pasta (see page 19), since you'll need that pasta as your vessel to hold the delicious fillings. You can experiment as you'd like with filling ideas, but the main thing you'll need is a binder. I generally use a vegan cheese of some kind. Ricotta may be the most popular, but mascarpone or other "smooth" cheeses work well too! In addition to the cheese, you can bring in an egg substitute (flax egg, chia egg, etc.) to help bind your filling together if it has trouble holding with cheese alone. You can also add just about any vegan meat, vegetable, or herb to your filling. While herbs can go in raw, I typically recommend cooking your "meat" or vegetables and allowing them to cool before adding them to your filling.

The key to making great filled pastas is making sure your pasta is *super* thin. You should be able to slightly see through the sheet of pasta if you hold it up to the light. Is there such a thing as too thin? Unfortunately, yes. But you will quickly get a feel for it, since when the pasta is too thin it will break while folding.

When it comes to filled pasta shapes, there's several shapes that you'll see in the next few pages that all range in difficulty when it comes to folding. Ravioli is the easiest, and they go up in difficulty from there. If you have trouble with everything beyond ravioli though, don't worry! Filled pasta should be something that is fun to make. Even ravioli are so impressive and gratifying when you serve them! With practice, you'll be an expert at all shapes of filled pasta.

When filling pasta, it's very important to make sure you're using the right ratios of filling to pasta. My grandma taught me that in most cases, a ratio of one-third filling to two-thirds dough is best, but you can experiment with different ratios. You can fill the pasta by placing the filling onto the pasta shape with a small spoon or you can transfer the filling to a piping bag and pipe the filling onto the pasta shape. Once you get better at folding certain shapes, you may enjoy packing them with a little more filling.

When folding any shape, it's very important to push any air out around the filling before sealing them; otherwise, they'll puff up or break while cooking. To seal them, you just need a little water brushed over the edge and then you can press them shut with your fingers or with a ravioli stamp or specialized tool. Once you have them filled and ready to go, I was always taught it's best to let them dry on the counter or in the fridge for around 30 minutes before cooking so they're a little more stable.

To cook the filled pasta, you simply place them in boiling salted water until they float! As far as sauces go, it's best to keep it to something light. You want the pasta to be the star of the show, of course. There are certain times where a heartier sauce would come into play, but for the most part, you'll want a lighter sauce. If you add a sauce like a hearty Bolognese or rich Alfredo, it might overpower the pasta. Going with something like a white wine or butter and herb sauce, which will complement the pasta, is typically the way to go!

BUTTERNUT SQUASH RAVIOLI WITH BROWN BUTTER, SAGE, AND CALABRIAN CHILE CANDIED HAZELNUTS

Butternut squash is a mellow but sweet flavor that pairs perfectly with brown butter and most anything spicy. This dish is semi-inspired by what I made when I was on a cooking show, where I made a butternut squash risotto with Sriracha candied hazelnuts. It tasted incredible. I wanted to translate that into ravioli, and this is what I came up with! Calabrian chile candied hazelnuts might sound a little strange at first, but the sweet and spicy crunch elegantly complements the squash.

Yield: 4 servings

Time: 30 minutes

INGREDIENTS:

1 cup (140 g) butternut squash

1 cup (250 g) vegan ricotta (see page 56 for recipe)

Salt to taste

8 vegan pasta sheets (see page 19 for recipe)

4 tablespoons (55 g) vegan butter (see page 40 for recipe)

1 large shallot

3 garlic cloves

10 to 14 sage leaves

1 cup (115 g) crushed hazelnuts

3 tablespoons (45 ml) maple syrup

1 tablespoon (14 g) Calabrian chiles

Grated vegan Parmesan (see page 51 for recipe)

METHOD:

1. Boil and cool the butternut squash and then use a potato masher or food processor to turn it into a smooth puree.

2. Mix the ricotta with the butternut squash puree and add salt to taste. Transfer to a piping bag.

3. Lay out four of the pasta sheets on a floured surface. Pipe about 1 tablespoon (15 ml) of filling 2 inches (5 cm) apart in two rows on each pasta sheet.

4. Lay the other four pasta sheets carefully over the top of the pasta sheets with filling on top and press around each pocket of filling to push any air out.

5. Using a ravioli cutter (in any shape), cut out the ravioli.

6. Boil the ravioli in a large pot of salted water until they float and then drain.

7. For the sauce, add the butter, shallot, garlic, and sage leaves to a large skillet and allow to cook over medium-low heat for 10 to 15 minutes until lightly browned and the sage leaves are crispy. Salt to taste and set aside.

Continued >

8. For the candied hazelnuts, add the hazelnuts, maple syrup, Calabrian chiles, and salt to a pot over medium heat. Once everything becomes sticky, spread out evenly on a piece of parchment paper to cool.

9. Check to make sure the pan with the sauce is still warm and get it warm if needed. Add the ravioli and swirl to combine.

10. Transfer to individual serving bowls and top with a sprinkling of the candied hazelnuts and Parmesan—and make sure each bowl gets a few of the crispy sage leaves.

BEET AND TARRAGON TORTELLINI

Beets aren't everyone's favorite vegetable, but adding them to your pasta dough is a subtle way to incorporate their flavor and color. The tarragon in the filling brings out the richness of the beets. It's delicious, and the look of the pink tortellini is stunning. It's visually impressive when plated—a perfect dish for a special occasion with that special someone.

Yield: 4 servings

Time: 30 minutes

INGREDIENTS:

1½ cups (375 g) vegan ricotta (see page 56 for recipe)

1 tablespoon (4 g) chopped fresh tarragon, plus more for serving

1 teaspoon lemon zest, plus more for serving

1 garlic clove, minced

4 beet-flavored vegan pasta sheets (see page 20 for recipe)

3 tablespoons (42 g) vegan butter (see page 40 for recipe)

1 shallot

Salt to taste

1 cup (235 ml) dry white wine

Juice of 1 lemon

1 cup (235 ml) reserved pasta water

METHOD:

1. In a mixing bowl, combine the ricotta with the tarragon, lemon zest, and minced garlic. Mix well to combine and transfer to a piping bag.

2. Lay the sheets of beet-flavored pasta out on a floured surface. Cut the sheets of pasta into 2-inch (5 cm) squares.

3. Pipe about 1 teaspoon of the ricotta mixture into the center of the square and fold one corner to the opposite, making a triangle. Push out the excess air and press the edges together to seal. Wrap the long edges of the filled pasta around your finger to form a ring. Press the points together to complete the tortellini shape.

4. For the sauce, add the butter and shallot to a skillet over medium heat, salting to taste.

5. Cook until the shallots are translucent, then add the white wine and lemon juice. Bring the mixture to a boil and then turn down the heat to the point where the mixture is at a gentle simmer and simmer until the liquid reduces by half.

6. While the sauce reduces, boil the tortellini in a large pot of salted water until they float. Once cooked, remove from the water, reserving 1 cup (235 ml) of pasta water.

7. Once the sauce has reduced, add the tortellini to the sauce along with a splash of pasta water.

8. As soon as everything is stirred and combined, transfer the tortellini and sauce to individual serving bowls, topping with more fresh tarragon and lemon zest if desired.

RICOTTA AND CHICKEN MEZZALUNE WITH MARSALA CREAM SAUCE

Mezzalune are ravioli that are shaped like a half-moon, which is where their name comes from. This dish is inspired by a restaurant in Buffalo, New York, except they paired theirs with a vodka sauce (which is also doable!). Growing up, I was a big fan of chicken marsala, and I wanted to combine both worlds with this recipe. Pairing the chicken-stuffed ravioli with the marsala cream sauce elevates the flavors and brings me back to sitting in leather-upholstered booths for my non-Italian grandmother's birthdays, since she loved marsala sauce more than anyone I know.

Yield: 4 servings

Time: 30 minutes

INGREDIENTS:

2 tablespoons (28 ml) olive oil

1 small yellow onion, finely chopped

3 garlic cloves, minced

1 cup (235 ml) marsala wine

1½ cups (366 g) vegan Alfredo sauce (see page 31 for recipe)

6 vegan pasta sheets (see page 19 for recipe)

1½ cups (375 g) vegan ricotta (see page 56 for recipe)

¼ teaspoon crushed red pepper

Salt to taste

1 vegan chicken cutlet, shredded (see page 67 for recipe)

Fresh basil

Grated vegan Parmesan (see page 51 for recipe)

METHOD:

1. For the sauce, add the olive oil, chopped onion, and garlic to a skillet over medium heat and cook for 5 minutes until soft and fragrant.

2. Add the marsala wine, bring the heat up to high, and cook until reduced by half.

3. Once the wine is reduced, add the Alfredo sauce, decrease the heat to low, and cook until thickened.

4. For the mezzalune, lay the pasta sheets out on a floured surface.

5. Cut circles out of them and set aside.

6. For the filling, mix together the ricotta, crushed red pepper, salt to taste, and shredded chicken.

7. Spoon about 1 to 2 teaspoons of filling onto the pasta sheets, fold in half, and crimp to seal the edges.

8. Boil the mezzalune in a large pot of salted water until they float and then transfer with a slotted spoon directly into the marsala cream sauce.

9. Plate, and then top with fresh basil and Parmesan.

SUN-DRIED TOMATO RICOTTA AGNOLOTTI WITH ASPARAGUS SAUCE

As a kid, I loved asparagus. One of my favorites was asparagus with sun-dried tomato pesto, which I was always going back to for seconds. While we aren't using pesto here, the sun-dried tomatoes in the agnolotti filling paired with a creamy asparagus sauce is visually stunning and reminds me of springtime lunches with my aunt on her farm.

Yield: 4 servings

Time: 30 minutes

INGREDIENTS:

2 cups (488 g) vegan Alfredo sauce (see page 31 for recipe)

1 tablespoon (15 ml) lemon juice

1 cup (180 g) chopped blanched asparagus

Sea salt to taste

1½ cups (375 g) vegan ricotta (see page 56 for recipe)

6 to 8 sun-dried tomatoes in oil

1 tablespoon (3 g) chopped fresh basil, plus more for serving

8 vegan pasta sheets (see page 19 for recipe)

METHOD:

1. For the sauce, in a food processor blend the Alfredo, lemon juice, blanched asparagus, and salt to taste. Add to a large skillet and warm over low heat.

2. For the filling, add the ricotta, sun-dried tomatoes, basil, and salt to taste to a food processor and blend until smooth. Transfer to a piping bag.

3. Lay out the pasta sheets and cut into 1 by 2-inch (2.5 by 5 cm) rectangles. Pipe about 2 teaspoons of filling on each rectangle and fold over into agnolotti.

4. Boil the agnolotti in a large pot of salted water until they float and then transfer with a slotted spoon directly into the sauce. Top with more fresh basil.

LEMON CAPPELLETTI
WITH PISTACHIO CREAM

Cappelletti is like the little cousin to tortellini, since they're smaller and folded slightly differently. The bright, citrusy flavor of the lemon with the pistachio cream is perfect for cappelletti because of its size and shape! I recommend making a double batch of this one since they're good even when you have them as leftovers.

Yield: 4 servings

Time: 30 minutes

INGREDIENTS:

1½ cups (375 g) vegan ricotta (see page 56 for recipe)

3 tablespoons (18 g) lemon zest, plus more for serving

¼ teaspoon crushed red pepper, plus more for serving

1 teaspoon chopped fresh thyme, plus more for serving

Salt to taste

3 tablespoons (42 g) vegan pistachio butter

Juice of half a lemon

1½ cups (355 ml) vegan heavy cream (see page 39 for recipe)

1 garlic clove, minced

8 vegan spinach-flavored pasta sheets (see page 20 for recipe)

Grated vegan Parmesan (see page 51 for recipe)

Crushed pistachios

METHOD:

1. For the filling, mix together the ricotta, lemon zest, crushed red pepper, thyme, and salt to taste. Transfer to a piping bag.

2. For the sauce, in a bowl mix the pistachio butter, lemon juice, heavy cream, garlic, and salt to taste until the pistachio butter mixes well with the cream.

3. Lay the pasta sheets out on a floured surface and cut into 2-inch (5 cm) circles.

4. Pipe about 1 teaspoon of filling on each circle and fold in half. Starting at the top, push out the excess air and press the edges together to seal. Wrap the long edges of the filled pasta around your finger to form a ring. Press the points together to complete the cappelletti shape.

5. Boil the cappelletti in a large pot of salted water until they float and then transfer with a slotted spoon directly into the sauce along with a small ladle of pasta water.

6. Transfer to individual serving bowls and top with Parmesan, crushed pistachios, and more crushed red pepper, lemon zest, and fresh thyme.

RAVIOLO AL' UOVO

The name of this dish basically means "giant egg raviolo"—and each one is double the size of your normal ravioli to accommodate for the filling. In a non-vegan kitchen, this is one of the most showstopping and technically difficult dishes to pull off. In a vegan kitchen, it's even harder and even more impressive since we're creating the "egg" yolk ourselves! This will be a test of everything you've learned so far, and it's 100 percent worth it. On its own, the ravioli already have so much flavor and don't need to be paired with an intricate sauce. The brown butter and sage are enough! This recipe is a rare one in the vegan world because of how uniquely non-vegan it looks and sounds at first, but with a little bit of love and effort, you'll be proud of yourself for serving this to your friends and family.

Yield: 4 servings
(2 or 3 ravioli per serving)

Time: 30 minutes

INGREDIENTS:

Egg yolk sauce from the Carbonara recipe (see page 123 for recipe)

1 cup (250 g) vegan ricotta (see page 56 for recipe)

2 tablespoons (6 g) finely chopped fresh basil

Salt and black pepper to taste

4 vegan pasta sheets (see page 19 for recipe)

4 tablespoons (55 g) vegan butter (see page 40 for recipe)

10 sage leaves

METHOD:

1. Make the egg yolk sauce and place into small molds (see page 59) and freeze.

2. For the ricotta filling, mix together the ricotta, basil, salt, and black pepper. Transfer to a piping bag.

3. Lay the pasta sheets out on a floured surface. On two of the pasta sheets, pipe 12 circles just larger than the size of a frozen yolk sauce cube. Place a frozen yolk sauce cube in the center of each circle. Lay the remaining pasta sheets on top and press down around the sides to push any air out. Cut each raviolo either round or square—about double or triple the size of typical ravioli. Press the edges to seal.

4. For the sauce, add the butter and sage leaves to a skillet over medium heat and cook for 10 to 15 minutes until browned and the sage is crispy.

5. Boil the ravioli in a large pot of salted water until they float and then transfer with a slotted spoon directly into the sauce. Add a little pasta water and gently swirl to coat.

6. Plate with extra browned butter and crispy sage leaves on top.

SQUID INK FAGOTTINI WITH BASIL GARLIC YOGURT

Fagottini look like miniature coin purses, and they're easy to make! The "squid ink" makes the pasta black, which is a visual treat. Instead of using a warm sauce, I created a vibrant, creamy sauce with herbaceous and tangy flavors from the basil and yogurt, respectively. This dish is ideal for a fancy pasta night, since it's gorgeous on the plate and bursting with unique flavor combinations.

Yield: 4 servings

Time: 30 minutes

INGREDIENTS:

1 tablespoon (14 g) vegan butter (see page 40 for recipe)

1 large cluster oyster mushrooms

1½ cups (375 g) vegan ricotta (see page 56 for recipe)

2 teaspoons lemon zest, plus more for serving

Salt to taste

8 vegan "squid ink" pasta sheets (see page 20 for recipe)

3 cups (690 g) plain vegan yogurt

4 garlic cloves

10 basil leaves, plus more for serving

Crushed red pepper to taste

METHOD:

1. For the filling, melt the butter in a skillet. Finely chop the mushrooms and cook them in the butter until golden brown, then season with salt to taste.

2. Let the mushrooms cool and then mix with the ricotta, lemon zest, and salt to taste. Transfer to a piping bag.

3. Lay the pasta out on a floured surface and cut into 2-inch (5 cm) squares. Pipe about 1 to 2 teaspoons of filling into the center. Moisten the outside edges of the pasta with a wet finger, then bring each corner up to the center of the square like a four-sided pyramid. Working from the bottom up, press the air out of the filling as you seal up the sides, creating the distinctive fagottini shape.

4. Boil the fagottini in a large pot of salted water until they float, then drain.

5. For the sauce, add the yogurt, garlic cloves, and basil leaves to a blender with salt to taste and blend until smooth.

6. To serve, swirl some of the yogurt sauce into a bowl, add some of the fagottini on top, and top with crushed red pepper and more lemon zest and fresh basil.

LOBSTER RAVIOLI WITH SAFFRON MASCARPONE CREAM

Lobster ravioli is one of the most popular forms of ravioli you'll find in Italian restaurants. However, thanks to lobster mushrooms, anyone eating this would be none the wiser. The saffron mascarpone cream is floral and sweet and complements the richness of the lobster mushroom. Topping with crispy, buttery garlic corn finishes this one off in a satisfying way that will make you not want to share these with anyone, even though you should!

Yield: 4 servings

Time: 30 minutes

INGREDIENTS:

1 pound (455 g) lobster mushrooms (or use oyster mushrooms if not available)

6 tablespoons (85 g) vegan butter, divided (see page 40 for recipe)

Salt and black pepper to taste

2 cups (500 g) vegan ricotta (see page 56 for recipe)

2 teaspoons lemon zest

8 vegan pasta sheets (see page 19 for recipe)

Juice of 1 lemon

1 teaspoon saffron

1 cup (240 g) vegan mascarpone (see page 60 for recipe)

1 cup (235 ml) vegan heavy cream (see page 39 for recipe)

1 cup (154 g) sweet corn

1 garlic clove, minced

Fresh basil

METHOD:

1. For the filling, start by finely chopping the mushrooms into tiny bits. Add 4 tablespoons (55 g) of butter to a skillet and cook the mushrooms with salt to taste until golden. Drain off excess butter and set aside to cool.

2. Once cooled, in a bowl, mix the mushrooms with the ricotta, lemon zest, and salt to taste. Transfer to a piping bag.

3. Take four of the pasta sheets and lay them out on a floured surface. Pipe about 1 tablespoon (15 ml) of filling 2 inches (5 cm) apart in two rows on each sheet. Lay the other sheets on top and press down around the filling to push any air out. Cut around the filling of each ravioli with a ravioli cutter.

4. For the sauce, in a skillet over medium heat, warm the lemon juice and add the saffron to bloom it. Add the mascarpone, heavy cream, and pepper and salt to taste and stir to combine.

5. Place the remaining 2 tablespoons (28 g) of butter in another skillet, add the corn and garlic, and cook until golden brown.

6. Boil the ravioli in a large pot of salted water until they float and then transfer with a slotted spoon directly into the sauce along with a small ladle of pasta water.

7. Transfer to a serving dish and top with the buttered corn and garlic and fresh basil.

Chapter 7

Breads and Spreads

HERBED SHALLOT AND HEIRLOOM TOMATO FOCACCIA

Focaccia is one of the best weapons in the arsenal of Italian cuisine. What sets it apart from other breads is the seemingly insane amount of olive oil that you cook the bread in, but it is worth it. All the olive oil makes the bread crispy and crunchy on the outside while keeping the inside fluffy and light. It's a wonderful bread for sandwiches because it adds a burst of flavor without weighing it down. Traditionally, focaccia is topped with flaky sea salt and herbs, primarily rosemary. You can top it with olives, cheese, or almost anything else you can think of. I love taking it fresh out of the oven and dipping it into quality balsamic vinegar or the Calabrian Chile Aioli on page 168. For this recipe, I listed the ingredients in weight measurements, which is the standard for bread recipes.

METHOD:

1. To make the poolish: Combine all the poolish ingredients in a large mixing bowl.

2. Mix until well combined with a wooden spoon and then cover tightly with a lid or plastic wrap. Let sit at room temperature for 8 to 12 hours, preferably until doubled in size.

3. To make the dough: Once the poolish has doubled in size, combine the poolish with the warm water, olive oil, agave, salt, and yeast.

4. Slowly add the bread flour and mix until well combined. Form into a rough ball, cover, and let rest at room temperature for 20 minutes.

5. Wet your hands with warm water and, keeping the dough in the bowl, lift the underside of the dough and pull it up and away until it seems like it's about to rip in half. Fold the dough back over the dough ball, then rotate the bowl. Do this about three more times until all sides of the dough have been brought into the center. Cover again and allow the dough to rest for 30 minutes.

6. Repeat the same stretching, folding, and resting process two more times. You'll notice a change in texture each time.

Yield: 8 to 10 servings

Time: 24 hours

INGREDIENTS:

POOLISH

175 grams (1¼ cups) bread flour

175 grams (¾ cup) lukewarm water

½ teaspoon instant yeast

NOTE: *Poolish is a highly fluid yeast-cultured mixture. It's a type of preferment used mostly in bread products.*

DOUGH

350 grams (12½ ounces) poolish

200 grams (¾ cup plus 1 tablespoon) water, warm to the touch

15 grams (1 tablespoon) olive oil, plus more as needed

4 grams agave

12 grams salt

¼ teaspoon instant yeast

300 grams (2¼ cups) bread flour

Continued >

7. After the last resting period, coat the inside of a clean bowl with olive oil. Place the dough into the bowl and cover with more olive oil—no need to be shy here. Cover the bowl tightly with plastic wrap or a lid and place in the refrigerator overnight.

8. Remove your dough from the refrigerator and allow it to come to room temperature. Generously coat a baking pan with olive oil on all sides and leave about ¼ inch (6 mm) of oil in the bottom of the pan. The size pan you use is up to you. You can use a smaller pan for a thicker focaccia or a larger pan for a thinner focaccia. A thicker focaccia will be soft and chewy, while a thinner focaccia will be crisper.

9. Transfer your room temperature dough to the pan, stretching it to fit without ripping. Cover the pan with a kitchen towel and place on the counter until it doubles in size.

10. Preheat the oven to 475°F (240°C, or gas mark 9).

11. Wet your hands with warm water and dimple the dough with your fingertips. You'll want to do this more than you think, because the dough will spring back. I usually do about eight to ten rounds of dimpling. If your focaccia is thick, it will take more dimpling than a thin one.

12. For the toppings: Drizzle the dough with a generous coat of olive oil—enough to fill in the dimples. Don't be scared—olive oil is what makes the bread so delicious!

13. Press the shallots, heirloom tomato, smashed garlic, and herbs into the dough all over, then generously sprinkle with flaky salt.

14. Place the baking tray in the oven on the top rack and bake for roughly 10 to 15 minutes. Rotate the pan 180 degrees and bake for another 10 to 15 minutes. Thick focaccia may take about 20 to 25 minutes per turn, while thin focaccia may take 7 to 10 minutes per turn. The top of your focaccia should be a deep golden brown color. If is it not, keep baking and rotating in 5-minute intervals.

15. Remove the focaccia from the oven and let cool for 5 minutes, then carefully transfer it from the baking pan to a wire rack over a baking sheet to cool. Take whatever excess olive oil is in the pan, drizzle it over the focaccia, and sprinkle over some more flaky salt.

16. Let cool for 15 to 20 minutes before cutting the focaccia to let the bread finish steaming. Slice up and enjoy.

TOPPINGS

35 grams (2 tablespoons plus 1 teaspoon) olive oil

2 shallots, thinly sliced

1 heirloom tomato, thinly sliced and wrapped in paper towel

10 to 12 garlic cloves, smashed

1 sprig fresh rosemary, destemmed

2 sprigs fresh thyme, destemmed

Flaky salt

NOTE:

Alternatively, in step 7, you can skip the cold fermentation and proof the dough for 1 hour on the counter in a warm area of your home. However, the slow, cold ferment makes the focaccia that much better.

ROASTED GARLIC BREAD

There's almost nothing better than garlic bread, especially when you make it with three different forms of garlic—roasted, minced, and powdered. Overboard? I don't think so, as each brings a unique dimension to the bread that you wouldn't get otherwise. I think it's the most delicious garlic bread you'll ever have, with cheese or without. At the least, it will definitely keep vampires at bay with the sheer amount of garlic!

Yield: 8 servings

Time: 20 minutes

INGREDIENTS:

1 cup (225 g) vegan butter (see page 40 for recipe)

2 heads roasted garlic (see page 44 for recipe)

3 garlic cloves, minced

1 teaspoon garlic powder

1 teaspoon salt

1 tablespoon (4 g) chopped fresh parsley

3 tablespoons (23 g) grated vegan Parmesan (see page 51 for recipe)

1 loaf of rustic Italian bread (see page 160 for recipe)

Fresh vegan mozzarella (see page 48 for recipe; optional)

METHOD:

1. Preheat the oven to 450°F (230°C, or gas mark 8).

2. Let the butter come to room temperature and then mix in the roasted garlic, minced garlic, garlic powder, salt, parsley, and Parmesan until well combined.

3. Slice the bread in half lengthwise and generously spread the garlic butter mixture over each half.

4. Place each piece of bread with the butter-side up on a baking tray.

   NOTE: *If you want to make cheesy garlic bread, this is where you should top with slices of fresh vegan mozzarella.*

5. Bake the bread on the middle shelf of the oven for 10 minutes and then broil for 1 to 2 minutes to get it extra golden on the top.

RUSTIC ITALIAN BREAD

Even if you are an expert bread maker, everyone needs that one easy bread that you can make without a Herculean amount of effort. This recipe is something I've been making since I was five years old, which means you can make it at home no problem. It pairs perfectly with any dish in this book and should be a staple of any Italian dinner table. This is your opportunity to use all those compound butters on page 43!

Yield: 2 loaves

Time: 2 hours 20 minutes

INGREDIENTS:

1¼ teaspoons
dry active yeast

1½ cups (355 ml)
lukewarm water, divided

1 teaspoon agave

4½ cups (563 g)
all-purpose flour, plus
a little extra for the top

1½ teaspoons salt

METHOD:

1. Dissolve the yeast in ¼ cup (60 ml) of warm water and stir in the agave.

2. Measure the flour into a large mixing bowl, add the dissolved yeast and the remaining 1¼ cups (295 ml) of water, and stir rapidly with a fork.

3. Add the salt and stir. The dough should be soft and sticky.

4. Sprinkle the surface with more flour, cover with plastic wrap, and let rise in a warm place for 1 hour and 30 minutes.

5. Preheat the oven to 430°F (220°C, or gas mark 7).

6. Transfer the dough to a floured board using a spatula (the floured surface must be facing up) and divide the dough into two loaves.

7. Gently transfer them to a nonstick baking sheet, sprinkled with flour.

8. Bake in the preheated oven for about 25 minutes and then lower the oven to 320°F (170°C, or gas mark 3) and bake for additional 10 to 15 minutes or until golden brown.

9. Cool on a wire rack for 20 minutes before cutting.

BRUSCHETTA

You can think of bruschetta like an Italian pico de gallo. It's fantastic on its own as a dip, and you can also pile it on top of chicken, add it to a charcuterie board, or spread it on toasted bread. It's one of the most versatile dishes you'll find in this book. My favorite way to eat it is to toast up a nice piece of bread, rub a garlic clove over the bread while it's still hot, and then top it with a hefty scoop of bruschetta and a little bit of the oil and juice at the bottom of the bowl you made the bruschetta in. If you're feeling extra fancy, you can drizzle some balsamic glaze over the top as well.

Yield: 10 servings

Time: 15 minutes

INGREDIENTS:

1 pint (550 g) cherry tomatoes

2 garlic cloves

¼ small red onion

2 teaspoons lemon zest

Juice of half a lemon

4 tablespoons (60 ml) extra-virgin olive oil

8 to 10 basil leaves, finely chopped

¾ teaspoon sea salt

1 teaspoon black pepper

METHOD:

1. Cut the tomatoes into quarters, mince the garlic, and very finely dice the red onion. Add them all to a mixing bowl.

2. Add the lemon zest, lemon juice, olive oil, basil, salt, and pepper. Mix well.

3. Cover and place in the fridge for at least an hour, although the longer this sits, the better! A decent amount of liquid will collect at the bottom of the bowl, but that's okay. (It's delicious for soaking up on a piece of crusty bread.)

4. Right before serving, give it a quick stir and top with more fresh basil.

CAPONATA

A Sicilian dish, caponata is a spread that you can put on all sorts of breads—or whatever you want, really! It's primarily made with eggplant, and I sometimes think of it as the "pantry cleanout" spread because it leans so heavily on common pantry ingredients. Don't worry, this doesn't make it any less delicious. Even some who claim they don't enjoy eggplant on its own may take to it. I feel like I've yet to find a person who doesn't enjoy a good caponata.

METHOD:

1. Chop the eggplant into small cubes and toss with 2 teaspoons of salt. Place in a colander and allow to sit for about 30 minutes to drain any liquid. Rinse the eggplant off and pat dry.

2. In a large skillet over medium-low heat, add 2 tablespoons (28 ml) of olive oil along with the celery, onion, and garlic. Cook for about 10 minutes until everything is nice and soft. Transfer to a mixing bowl using a slotted spoon and set aside.

   NOTE: *When the vegetables cook in this recipe, I do sometimes partially cover the pan with a lid to capture steam and prevent browning.*

3. Heat the remaining 2 tablespoons (28 ml) of olive oil in the same skillet, turn the heat up to medium, and add the eggplant. Cook, stirring constantly, for 5 to 7 minutes until golden.

4. Add the celery and onion mix back in with the eggplant, along with the tomatoes, olives, capers, tomato paste, and oregano. Bring the mixture to a boil and then reduce the heat to low and cook, uncovered, for about 15 minutes until it has thickened to the point where there's no excess liquid. Stir frequently.

5. Take the pan off the heat and add the vinegar, sugar, remaining 1 teaspoon of salt, and pepper.

6. Transfer to a serving bowl and top with the fresh parsley.

Yield: 16 servings

Time: 1 hour 30 minutes

INGREDIENTS:

1 eggplant, peeled

3 teaspoons (18 g) salt, divided

¼ cup (60 ml) olive oil, divided

1 cup (120 g) finely diced celery

1 red onion, finely diced

2 garlic cloves, minced

1½ cups (363 g) canned whole tomatoes, drained and chopped

15 green olives, pitted and chopped

1½ tablespoons (14 g) capers, drained

1 tablespoon (16 g) tomato paste

1 teaspoon minced fresh oregano

2 tablespoons (28 ml) red wine vinegar

2 teaspoons organic cane sugar

1 teaspoon black pepper

2 teaspoons minced fresh parsley

FRESH BASIL PESTO AND SUN-DRIED TOMATO PESTO

This is a two-in-one recipe because they're identical save for the sun-dried tomatoes, which add a rich, sweet flavor to the base pesto. Traditionally, pesto sauces are made with a mortar and pestle—if you're having a stressful day, this is the perfect recipe to work out some of that frustration! These pestos are wonderful as a dip for bread, sandwich spread, and on top different vegan meats. You can also toss them with pasta or use them as the base on a homemade pizza.

Yield: 1 cup (260 g) pesto

Time: 20 minutes

INGREDIENTS:

BASIL PESTO

2 large garlic cloves

⅓ teaspoon sea salt

¼ cup (35 g) pine nuts

¼ cup (30 g) grated vegan Parmesan (see page 51 for recipe)

4 cups (96 g) tightly packed fresh basil leaves

1 tablespoon (15 ml) lemon juice

1 teaspoon lemon zest

1 teaspoon black pepper

¾ cup (175 ml) extra-virgin olive oil

SUN-DRIED TOMATO PESTO

1 cup (260 g) Basil Pesto

½ cup (55 g) sun-dried tomatoes in oil, drained

METHOD:

BASIL PESTO

1. In a mortar and pestle, add the garlic and salt. Mash into a paste and then add the pine nuts and Parmesan. Continue to mash and grind until the nuts and cheese have broken down to a fine consistency.

2. Add the basil, lemon juice and zest, and pepper. Mash very well until the basil has become a paste with the rest of the ingredients.

3. Add the olive oil in 1 tablespoon (15 ml) increments, making sure to mash very well between each addition to help emulsify the pesto.

SUN-DRIED TOMATO PESTO

1. Once the Basil Pesto is prepared as above, remove from the mortar and pestle and set aside. Add the sun-dried tomatoes to the mortar and pestle. Mash them up into a paste.

2. Add the Basil Pesto back into the mashed tomatoes and mix well until combined.

NOTES:

• *If you don't have a mortar and pestle or don't feel comfortable using one, you can use a food processor. For the emulsification of the oil, just drizzle it in at the end while the processor is on.*

• *For the Sun-Dried Tomato Pesto, when making the base pesto, feel free to use the olive oil that the sun-dried tomatoes come in, instead of extra-virgin olive oil (or do half and half) to amp up the tomato flavor.*

CALABRIAN CHILE AIOLI

Not everyone is a fan of heat for the sake of heat, but adding Calabrian chiles to mayo and making a simple aioli is an easy way to make it palatable for the weak. Just kidding: You can use this wonderful creation as a dip, spread it on a sandwich, and it pairs well with a variety of dishes. Calabrian chiles are pretty spicy but so delicious—they have a unique sweet and floral note. I like to use it as a dipping sauce for the Mozzarella Fritta (see page 199) or spread it over some freshly out-of-the-oven focaccia (see page 156). I recommend doubling or tripling this recipe so you can have some saved for later because you're going to want to put it on everything.

Yield: 12 servings

Time: 10 minutes

INGREDIENTS:

1 block (16 ounces, or 455 g) silken tofu, drained

1 block (16 ounces, or 455 g) firm tofu, drained

1 tablespoon (15 ml) lemon juice

2 teaspoons rice vinegar

2 teaspoons sea salt

1 to 4 tablespoons (14 to 56 g) chopped Calabrian chiles (depending on the desired spice level)

NOTE: *For this recipe and most times, I use Calabrian chiles packed in oil.*

METHOD:

1. Place all the ingredients in a blender and blend until smooth.

2. Transfer to a mason jar and keep in the fridge up to 1 week.

Chapter 8

Sides and Staples

FENNEL GRATIN

This dish is cooked in much the same way as potatoes au gratin; you're essentially making the core of the same dish—but with fennel! Fennel is a tender root vegetable with a strong black licorice flavor when eaten raw, but when it's cooked, it becomes a sweet and savory vegetable that works with almost anything. It's an amazing palate cleanser, and the flavor of the fennel makes the dish feel less heavy than it would otherwise.

METHOD:

1. Preheat the oven to 400°F (200°C, or gas mark 6).

2. Remove the stalks and fronds from the bulbs of fennel. (Discard the stalks but reserve the fronds for later.) Remove the outer layer from a fennel bulb, cut a "v" shape to remove the core, and cut it into wedges. Repeat for the other bulbs.

3. Place the fennel in a 9 by 13-inch (23 by 33 cm) baking dish and cover with the white wine and soy milk. Season to taste with salt and pepper and scatter the diced butter over the top.

4. Cover the baking dish with foil and bake on the center rack in the oven for 30 minutes or until the fennel is fork tender.

5. While the fennel cooks, make the topping. Mix together the melted butter, breadcrumbs, and Parmesan, adding salt and pepper to taste. Mix well.

6. Remove the baking dish from the oven and increase the oven temperature to 450°F (230°C, or gas mark 8). Sprinkle the topping over the fennel and return it to the oven once it hits 450°F (230°C, or gas mark 8).

7. Bake uncovered for 20 minutes or until the breadcrumbs are golden brown. Remove the dish from the oven. Top with the lemon zest and about 1 tablespoon (9 g) of chopped reserved fennel fronds. Serve while warm!

Yield: 6 to 8 servings

Time: 1 hour

INGREDIENTS:

3 fennel bulbs

⅓ cup (80 ml) white wine

½ cup (120 ml) plain unsweetened soy milk

Salt and black pepper to taste

3 tablespoons (42 g) vegan butter, diced (see page 40 for recipe)

3 tablespoons (42 g) vegan butter, melted (see page 40 for recipe)

¾ cup (90 g) breadcrumbs

1 cup (120 g) grated vegan Parmesan (see page 51 for recipe)

2 teaspoons lemon zest

WILD MUSHROOM AND SAGE RISOTTO

Mushroom risotto is one of the most popular types of risotto, at least according to the number of times I've seen it. I don't know why everyone decided that mushrooms are the best option, but they do seem to work well with risotto. After all, I'm not the biggest fan of mushrooms, but this recipe is an exception to the rule. I've found that crisping up the mushrooms with sage, garlic, and other spices and then adding them on top of the risotto adds more texture and flavor than if you simply mixed the mushrooms in. The sage and walnuts also give it that extra little something. Risotto is often seen as an intimidating dish to create, but it's just a little time-consuming. There's nothing to be afraid of here!

Yield: 4 to 6 servings

Time: 30 minutes

INGREDIENTS:

4 cups (950 ml) vegan chicken broth

3 tablespoons (42 g) vegan butter (see page 40 for recipe), divided

6 tablespoons (60 ml) olive oil, divided

1 shallot, finely diced

1 garlic clove, minced

1 cup (180 g) Arborio rice

1 cup (235 ml) dry white wine

1 teaspoon sea salt, divided

¼ cup (30 g) grated vegan Parmesan (see page 51 for recipe)

½ cup vegan heavy cream (see page 39 for recipe)

1 pound (455 g) wild mushrooms, chopped

2 tablespoons (6 g) chopped fresh sage

Chopped walnuts

METHOD:

1. In a pot over medium heat, add the chicken broth and bring to a simmer.

2. In a different pot, add 1 tablespoon each (14 g) of butter and (15 ml) olive oil and add the shallot and garlic. Cook for 3 to 4 minutes over medium heat until slightly translucent and fragrant.

3. Add the dry rice and toast until lightly golden brown.

4. Add the wine and ½ teaspoon of sea salt. Stir and increase the heat until the wine reduces by half and is starting to be absorbed by the rice.

5. Add a ladle of chicken broth at a time while stirring consistently over medium heat. When the rice looks like it has absorbed 90 percent of the liquid, add another ladleful. Repeat this process until the rice is tender.

6. Once tender, turn the heat to low and add the remaining 2 tablespoons (28 g) of butter, Parmesan, and heavy cream. Stir and cook until thick.

7. For the mushrooms, get a cast-iron skillet hot over high heat and add the remaining 3 tablespoons (45 ml) of olive oil, chopped wild mushrooms, remaining ½ teaspoon of salt, and chopped sage. Lay them out in a single layer in the pan and let them do their thing for a few minutes until nice and crisp and then flip!

8. Top the risotto with the mushrooms and chopped walnuts.

INSALATA MISTA WITH LEMON POPPY SEED VINAIGRETTE

This is one of my favorite salads, and the credit goes to a restaurant I grew up going to in Buffalo, New York, called Falletta's. We would go there on a weekly basis, and this is the salad that you would get no matter what you ordered on the menu. The dressing makes this particular dish because it's so bright that it enhances the flavors of the otherwise simple ingredients in the salad. I could probably drink the dressing on its own if it were socially acceptable.

Yield: 4 to 6 servings

Time: 10 minutes

INGREDIENTS:

½ cup (120 ml) fresh squeezed lemon juice

4 tablespoons (48 g) organic cane sugar

4 tablespoons (60 ml) extra-virgin olive oil

1½ tablespoons (14 g) poppy seeds

1 teaspoon minced garlic

1½ tablespoons (23 g) Dijon mustard

½ teaspoon salt

1 teaspoon black pepper

½ teaspoon onion powder

1 bag (5 ounces, or 140 g) spring mix salad mix, washed

Persian cucumbers, thinly sliced

Red onion, thinly sliced

METHOD:

1. In a mason jar, add the lemon juice, sugar, olive oil, poppy seeds, garlic, Dijon mustard, salt, pepper, and onion powder. Shake very well until emulsified.

2. In a large mixing bowl, add the spring mix and the thinly sliced cucumbers and red onion. Take a paper towel and get it damp with cold water and completely cover the salad without the dressing. Place in the fridge for 10 minutes to help crisp everything up.

3. Remove the paper towel, lightly season the vegetables with salt and pepper, and toss with the dressing right before serving.

"MY FAVORITE SOUP"

It's all in the name. This is a soup that my grandmother invented, and somehow nobody could even remember what it was called before literally everyone started calling it that. Growing up relatively poor, when it was her turn to make dinner for the family, she made this soup because she could stretch her ingredients by making tiny meatballs and including them in the soup. It's these little meatballs that are the special, not-so-secret ingredient, which really does something to your brain when you're eating them. It's hard to even explain, so you'll have to try it yourself and then track me down and confirm to me that it's your new favorite soup now too.

Yield: 6 to 8 servings

Time: 30 minutes

INGREDIENTS:

2 large carrots, diced

1 medium yellow onion, diced

2 large ribs celery, diced

2 tablespoons (28 ml) olive oil

Salt and black pepper, to taste

6 cups (1.4 L) vegan beef broth

1 can (14 ounces, or 390 g) tomato puree

½ pound (225 g) vegan ground beef (see page 64 for recipe)

1 tablespoon (4 g) chopped fresh Italian parsley, plus more for serving

1 pound (455 g) orzo

Grated vegan Parmesan (see page 51 for recipe)

METHOD:

1. Add all the vegetables to a stockpot with the olive oil. Season with salt and pepper and cook for 3 to 5 minutes over medium heat until they start to sweat, but not brown.

2. Add the beef broth, cover, and cook for 20 minutes at a simmer until the vegetables are tender. Add the tomato puree and stir to combine.

3. For the meatballs, mix together the ground beef, parsley, and salt and pepper to taste. To help them keep their shape while cooking, place the meatballs in the freezer for about 20 minutes. Then, drop them into the soup to cook. There's no need to brown them prior. Cook for 5 to 10 minutes at a low boil.

4. In a separate pot of boiling salted water, cook the orzo and then drain. Once the meatballs are warm and cooked through, take a serving bowl and add a scoop of orzo to the bottom and top with the meatball soup. Top with Parmesan and more fresh parsley if desired.

CAESAR SALAD WITH BACON

Best served as an appetizer, everyone loves a good Caesar salad. It can also be spiced up and upgraded to a bigger dish by adding a grilled vegan chicken cutlet. When my grandmother would make hers, she would top it with bacon or pancetta. Feel free to experiment with different ingredients in addition to the ones listed here to find out what you like best. Who knows, it might even become one of your signature dishes one day.

METHOD:

1. To make the croutons: Preheat the oven to 400°F (200°C, or gas mark 6).

2. In a large bowl, toss the cubed day-old bread with the olive oil, salt, and pepper to coat evenly. Transfer to a baking tray lined with parchment paper in an even single layer and place in the preheated oven for about 10 to 15 minutes, flipping halfway through, until golden brown and crisp.

3. To make the dressing: In a blender, blend all of the ingredients except for the pepper until smooth. Add that in last and stir to combine with a spoon.

4. To make the salad: Wash and dry the romaine and chop into bite-size pieces. Add to a serving bowl and top with the crumbled bacon, Parmesan shreds, homemade croutons, and Caesar dressing.

Yield: 4 to 6 servings

Time: 15 minutes

INGREDIENTS:

CROUTONS

2 cups (100 g) cubed day-old bread (see page 160 for recipe)

4 tablespoons (60 ml) olive oil

Salt and black pepper to taste

DRESSING

1 tablespoon (15 g) smooth Dijon mustard

½ teaspoon rice vinegar

1 tablespoon (15 ml) olive oil

1 tablespoon (21 g) agave

1 tablespoon (15 ml) soy sauce

2 tablespoons (22 g) nutritional yeast

½ cup (115 g) vegan mayonnaise

1 garlic clove

2 teaspoons capers

1½ tablespoons (25 ml) lemon juice

½ tablespoon caper brine

Salt to taste and lots of black pepper (about 2 teaspoons)

SALAD

3 heads romaine lettuce

½ cup (40 g) crumbled vegan bacon (see page 69 for recipe)

Shaved vegan Parmesan (see page 51 for recipe)

ROASTED BROCCOLINI WITH
LEMON GOAT CHEESE DRESSING

This dressing is something my grandmother used to make that we would literally just dip bread in and eat. In life, I started using it as a sauce for leftover vegetables, and one day, I threw it on some roasted broccolini and was impressed with the results. It's an awesome way to get your kids to eat vegetables because the cheesy sauce masks whatever flavors they might not like otherwise. It just makes every vegetable better!

Yield: 4 to 6 servings

Time: 25 minutes

INGREDIENTS:

2 big bunches broccolini

2 to 3 tablespoons
(28 to 45 ml) olive oil

Salt and black pepper
to taste

1 to 2 teaspoons
crushed red pepper

2 teaspoons minced garlic

1 cup (224 g) vegan goat
cheese (see page 55
for recipe)

2 teaspoons lemon zest

1 tablespoon (15 ml)
lemon juice

Water as needed

METHOD:

1. Preheat the oven to 450°F (230°C, or gas mark 8).

2. Cut the broccolini into approximately 1-inch (2.5 cm) pieces. I roast the stems and the leaves as well. In a large bowl, toss them with the olive oil, salt and black pepper, crushed red pepper, and minced garlic and spread in a single layer on a baking tray.

3. Place the broccolini in the oven and allow to cook for 10 to 15 minutes, flipping halfway. I like mine to still be crunchy, but for a softer texture, leave it in longer.

4. Place the goat cheese, lemon zest, lemon juice, and salt to taste in a food processor. Process until smooth and add water if needed. This should be the consistency of yogurt and should be able to be drizzled over the broccolini.

5. Serve the goat cheese dressing either on the side or drizzled on top of the freshly roasted broccolini.

CAPRESE SALAD

This tasty salad is also one of the easiest to make. If you're even the smallest bit Italian, I'm sure you're already very familiar with this one because it's a staple in most Italian households as a light introduction before the main course. It can also serve as a nice palate cleanser while the rest of the meal is being cooked. It's the perfect combo of creamy, tangy, and salty all in one!

Yield: 4 servings

Time: 5 minutes

INGREDIENTS:

2 cups (475 ml) balsamic vinegar

2 large balls fresh vegan mozzarella (see page 48 for recipe)

2 ripe Roma tomatoes

20 to 24 large basil leaves

2 tablespoons (28 ml) extra-virgin olive oil

Flaky sea salt and freshly cracked black pepper to taste

METHOD:

1. In a saucepot over medium-low heat, add the balsamic vinegar. Cook, stirring frequently, for about 30 minutes until it has thickened into a glaze. Allow to cool overnight before using.

2. Slice the mozzarella and tomatoes and plate by alternating a slice of tomato, a basil leaf, and a slice of mozzarella. Continue that pattern until all of the ingredients are used.

3. Drizzle some of the balsamic glaze and olive oil on top and sprinkle with some flaky sea salt and freshly cracked black pepper. Serve immediately.

PASTINA

My grandmother used to make this whenever I was sick. It's essentially the Italian chicken noodle soup, minus the chicken in our case! There's something special about the tiny, slightly overcooked pasta mixed with vegan chicken broth, butter, and Parmesan that makes you instantly feel better. You can use any type of tiny pasta for this dish, but stellini is what I recommend. It's also great for kids because they're in fun star shapes!

Yield: 8 to 10 servings

Time: 20 minutes

INGREDIENTS:

6 to 8 cups (1.4 to 1.9 L) vegan chicken broth

Salt to taste

4 garlic cloves, minced

1 pound (455 g) stellini

1¼ cups (175 g) frozen peas and carrots

4 tablespoons (55 g) vegan butter (see page 40 for recipe)

Grated vegan Parmesan (see page 51 for recipe)

Crushed red pepper (optional)

METHOD:

1. In a large pot over high heat, add the chicken broth, salt to taste, and minced garlic. Bring to a boil.

2. Once boiling, add the stellini and overcook by about 1 minute.

3. About 2 minutes before the stellini is overcooked, add the frozen vegetables and butter. Stir to combine.

4. Transfer to individual serving bowls and top with Parmesan and crushed red pepper if desired.

PASTA E CECI

"Ceci" means chickpea in Italian, and they make for a cheap and easy meal that tastes like a million bucks. Seriously, it tastes like you've been toiling over a stove for four days straight perfecting the taste of this thing. It's not quite a straight-up pasta dish, and it's not quite a soup. It's this middle ground of being a brothy pasta that's perfect for winter months or for when you're feeling a little under the weather.

Yield: 4 servings

Time: 25 minutes

METHOD:

1. Heat the olive oil in a large saucepan over medium heat. Add the onion and season with salt. Cook for about 5 minutes until the onion is soft. Add the garlic and continue to cook, stirring occasionally, until the onion and garlic are brown around the edges, 5 to 6 minutes more.

2. Add the rosemary (the whole sprigs) and crushed red pepper and cook, stirring, until fragrant. Add the chickpeas and tomatoes and cook until the tomatoes are slightly thickened, about 6 minutes.

3. Add the calamarata and water. Increase the heat to medium-high, bring to a simmer, and cook until the pasta is al dente, about 14 minutes. Stir in the parsley and Parmesan and season with salt to taste.

4. Divide among individual serving bowls. Drizzle with more olive oil and top with Parmesan and pepper.

INGREDIENTS:

¼ cup (60 ml) olive oil, plus more for serving

2 small onions, finely chopped

Sea salt to taste

6 garlic cloves, thinly sliced

2 sprigs rosemary

½ teaspoon crushed red pepper

2 cans (15 ounces, or 425 g each) chickpeas, drained, rinsed

2 cups (484 g) whole peeled tomatoes, crushed

12 ounces (340 g) calamarata

4 cups (946 ml) water

¼ cup (15 g) finely chopped fresh parsley

¼ cup (30 g) grated vegan Parmesan (see page 51 for recipe), plus more for serving

Freshly ground black pepper

ROSEMARY AND CITRUS MARINATED OLIVES

These olives are a delicious addition to a charcuterie board because they add brightness to an otherwise heavy dish. If you don't necessarily love olives, don't fret—the rosemary and citrus help cut through the briny flavor that olives tend to have. Another way to eat these is to chop them up and throw them on top of a Chicken Milanese (see page 203) or even make them into an olive tapenade you can spread over a slice of your favorite bread.

Yield: 10 to 12 servings

Time: Prep 10 minutes; Setting time 1 week

INGREDIENTS:

4 cups (720 g) green or kalamata olives

Extra-virgin olive oil (enough to cover the olives in the jar)

¼ cup (60 ml) red wine vinegar

2 sprigs fresh rosemary (stemmed and coarsely chopped)

3 garlic cloves, thinly sliced

1 teaspoon black pepper

2 to 4 dried chiles (depending on the desired spice level)

1 teaspoon fresh thyme

1 bay leaf

1 teaspoon fennel seeds

Juice and zest of 1 lemon

METHOD:

1. Mix the olive oil, vinegar, spices, herbs, and lemon juice and zest in a bowl until well combined.

2. Place the olives in a jar and cover with the oil mixture. Seal well and let sit for at least a week in the fridge. Serve with some crusty bread and goat cheese for maximum flavor results!

ENGLISH PEA ARANCINI

Arancini are deep-fried risotto balls, and a good way to use any risotto you have left over. You can add whatever you want to them, and my favorite way to make them is with peas and pesto. You can add mushrooms, extra cheese, or almost anything you're craving. They're fun to serve at parties because you don't see them very often, and they're sure to be an instant hit at family gatherings.

Yield: 8 to 10 servings

Time: 1 hour

INGREDIENTS:

1 batch Risotto
(see page 175 for recipe,
just skip the mushrooms
and toppings)

1 cup (130 g) frozen peas

Dredging Station (see
page 36 for instructions)

Oil for frying

Heirloom Pomodoro
Sauce (see page 32
for recipe)

Fresh parsley

METHOD:

1. While making the risotto, add the frozen peas at the same time as the heavy cream.

2. In an airtight container, add the risotto and spread evenly in a flat layer. Cover and place in the fridge overnight.

3. Take the cold risotto and scoop 2 to 3 tablespoons (15 to 45 g) of it and roll into a ball. Dredge them in breadcrumbs via the dredging station and place back in the fridge for 10 minutes.

4. Heat the oil to 375°F (190°C) in a deep stockpot or a deep fryer. Take the risotto balls and fry until golden brown, about 4 to 5 minutes. Remove and transfer to a paper towel and season with salt.

5. Make the Heirloom Pomodoro Sauce for dipping, top everything with fresh parsley, and serve!

NOTES:

• *You can add pesto to the risotto to add even more flavor!*

• *You can pair these with whatever sauce of your choosing, even Calabrian Chile Aioli (see page 168 for recipe)!*

STUFFED BANANA PEPPERS

These were a staple in my household growing up—we had them every Sunday! They're not overly spicy, and they're filled with the creamiest and most delicious cheese filling. It's a very popular dish for Italians in Buffalo, and it was a favorite of my grandmother's. Her pro tip was to always save the oil that you used to cook the peppers in and use it to dip bread because it turns into this incredible banana pepper oil. Out of any recipe in this book, this is a contender for my favorite because of how nostalgic and addicting it is for me.

Yield: 12 to 14 peppers (4 to 6 servings)

Time: 20 minutes

INGREDIENTS:

16 ounces (455 g) vegan ricotta, at room temperature (see page 56 for recipe)

1 cup (115 g) Italian breadcrumbs

8 ounces (225 g) shredded vegan mozzarella (see page 52 for recipe)

⅔ cup (80 g) grated vegan Parmesan (see page 51 for recipe)

3 tablespoons (30 g) minced garlic

Salt and black pepper to taste

12 to 14 banana peppers

Olive oil as needed

METHOD:

1. In a large bowl, mix the room temperature ricotta, breadcrumbs, mozzarella, Parmesan, minced garlic, and salt and pepper to taste until completely smooth and well combined.

2. Cut the tops off the peppers and carefully deseed them.

3. Place the cheese mixture into a piping bag and fill each pepper with the mix. Place the peppers in the fridge for 20 minutes.

4. In a deep skillet over medium heat, add enough olive oil to cover about one-quarter of the pepper's height.

5. Once the oil is shimmering, add the banana peppers to the pan, with space in between (this may have to be done in batches). Once the pepper is golden brown, about 4 to 5 minutes, flip and cook an additional few minutes to get the other side golden brown.

6. Remove from the pan and place on a paper towel to drain excess oil. Salt immediately coming out of the pan.

7. Let them rest for about a minute to set and then serve!

CALAMARI

Calamari is traditionally chopped squid that's breaded and deep-fried, usually served with marinara sauce. It's both an Italian and an Italian American dish, with the main difference being the way you bread it. For me, calamari wasn't something I ate very often before going vegan, but it was one of the few seafood dishes I enjoyed (likely because of the breading and marinara sauce). My grandmother loved making it for holidays and parties. She made it the Italian way, and my aunts and uncles would make it the Italian American way (which she never approved of). For me, the latter won out, so the recipe you see here is for the Italian American version. Sorry, Grandma!

Yield: 8 to 10 servings

Time: 30 minutes

INGREDIENTS:

Dredging Station (see page 36 for instructions)

Oil for frying

3 cans (14 ounces, or 390 g each) hearts of palm, rinsed and drained

Salt to taste

Heirloom Pomodoro Sauce (see page 32 for recipe)

Fresh parsley

Lemon wedges

METHOD:

1. Set up the dredging station and preheat the oil to 375°F (190°C) in a deep stockpot or deep fryer.

2. Take the hearts of palm, push out the centers to create rings, and slice about ¼ to ½ inch (6 to 13 mm) thick.

3. Bread the rings and centers in the dredging station and fry until golden brown, about 4 to 5 minutes.

4. Remove from the fryer (fry in batches) and place on a plate lined with a paper towel and season with salt right as they come out of the fryer.

5. Serve with Heirloom Pomodoro Sauce or any other desired sauce and top everything with fresh parsley and lemon wedges!

MOZZARELLA FRITTA

You've probably had mozzarella sticks at some point in your life, either from the local pizzeria or at a county fair. The difference here is that you're using fresh mozzarella instead of just frying up some string cheese and calling it a day. You'll want to make these super crispy and golden brown, and the cheese should ooze out when you bite into them. They'll probably be gone before you're even done cooking them if you have particularly snack-oriented friends or family.

Yield: 6 to 8 servings

Time: 45 minutes

INGREDIENTS:

4 balls fresh vegan mozzarella (see page 48 for recipe)

2 cups (230 g) Italian seasoned breadcrumbs

⅓ cup (40 g) grated vegan Parmesan (see page 51 for recipe), plus more for serving

1 tablespoon (4 g) dried parsley

Salt to taste

2 cups (475 ml) plain unsweetened soy milk

2¼ cups (280 g) all-purpose flour, divided

Canola oil for deep frying

Vegan tomato sauce for dipping (see page 27 or 32)

Fresh parsley

METHOD:

1. Take the mozzarella balls and either slice into rounds or sticks. Then, lay on a parchment-lined plate or tray in a single layer and place in the freezer for about 30 minutes.

2. In one bowl, mix together the breadcrumbs, Parmesan, dried parsley, and salt to taste.

3. In a second bowl, combine the soy milk, ¼ cup (30 g) of flour, and salt to taste.

4. In a third bowl, mix together the remaining 2 cups (250 g) of all-purpose flour with salt to taste.

5. Heat the canola oil to 375°F (190°C, or gas mark 5) in a heavy-bottomed stockpot.

6. Take the mozzarella out of the freezer and fully coat it in the flour first, then the soy milk mixture, and then the breadcrumbs. Really press the breadcrumbs in and make sure they're fully coating the cheese. Repeat until all are coated.

7. Deep fry in batches for 2 to 4 minutes or until golden brown. Transfer to a wire rack to drain and season with fine salt right when they come out of the fryer. Repeat until all are fried.

8. Serve with tomato sauce for dipping and top with Parmesan and fresh parsley if desired.

CHICKEN PARMESAN

This is very much an Italian American dish. It's one of my favorites though, and I needed to share my personal recipe with you all. It's the best vegan chicken parm you'll ever have. Not to brag; it's just the facts. There's everything to love about this dish—it's breaded and fried "chicken," coated in sauce and "cheese." No animals harmed.

Yield: 4 servings

Time: 30 minutes

INGREDIENTS:

Dredging Station (see page 36 for instructions)

Olive oil for a shallow fry

4 vegan chicken cutlets (see page 67 for recipe)

Salt to taste

Heirloom Pomodoro Sauce (see page 32 for recipe)

Shredded vegan mozzarella (see page 52 for recipe)

Fresh parsley

METHOD:

1. Set up the dredging station and start heating about ¼ inch (6 mm) of olive oil in a skillet over medium-high heat.

2. Take the chicken cutlets and dredge them as instructed in the dredging station recipe. Fry the breaded cutlets in the olive oil for about 2 to 3 minutes per side until golden brown.

3. Remove from the oil and place on a plate lined with a paper towel. Season with salt right as they come out.

4. Place the cutlets on a baking tray and top with Heirloom Pomodoro Sauce and shredded mozzarella. Place under the broiler until the cheese is melty and golden brown.

5. Top with fresh parsley and serve with a salad, pasta, or on its own!

CHICKEN MILANESE

This dish is incredibly versatile because it can be the base of many other recipes. It's also delicious on its own, and it's a light "chicken" dish that can be served with virtually any pasta, side dish, and more. It's sort of the Italian "chicken" nugget. You know you've got it right if it's perfectly golden brown and crispy!

Yield: 2 to 4 servings

Time: 30 minutes

INGREDIENTS:

4 vegan chicken cutlets (see page 67 for recipe)

Dredging Station (see page 36 for instructions)

1 cup (235 ml) olive oil

Arugula

Lemon wedges

METHOD:

1. Take the chicken cutlets and flatten them out.

2. Set up the dredging station (see page 36).

3. Take the chicken cutlets and coat them as instructed in the dredging station.

4. Once coated, place the chicken cutlets on a cutting board and gently roll with a rolling pin to really press the breadcrumbs in there. Add to a plate, separating each cutlet with a piece of parchment paper, and place in the fridge for 10 to 15 minutes.

5. Heat the olive oil in a skillet over medium/medium-high heat until shimmering..

6. Add the cutlets to the oil and cook for about 3 to 4 minutes per side until golden brown. Don't overcrowd the pan; make sure there's space between each cutlet.

7. Remove from the oil and place on a wire rack over a baking tray to drain. Immediately sprinkle each cutlet with salt. Serve with a bed of arugula piled on top and plenty of lemon wedges.

Resources

While I encourage you to try the recipes in this book for homemade ingredients (meats, cheeses, butters, etc.), sometimes pasta night can only happen if you lean on some store-bought substitutes! Here you'll find my recommendations for go-to vegan products.

MEATS

Ground meats

- Impossible
- Beyond Meat (with the casings removed)
- Gardein
- Cacique
- The Herbivorous Butcher
- Alpha Foods

Bacon

- Sweet Earth Enlightened Foods
- Lightlife
- BeLeaf
- Hooray Foods
- The Herbivorous Butcher

Chicken

- Gardein (Chick'n Scallopini; Chick'n Strips)
- Tofurky (Chick'n)

Sausages

- Field Roast Meat & Cheese Co.
- Tofurky
- Beyond Meat
- The Herbivorous Butcher

Deli meats

- Yves Veggie Cuisine
- Tofurky
- Field Roast Meat & Cheese Co.

CHEESES

Shreds

- Violife!
- Follow Your Heart
- Field Roast Meat & Cheese Co.
- Moocho
- Daiya

Slices

- Follow Your Heart
- Violife!
- Field Roast Meat & Cheese Co.

Other "artisanal" cheeses (such as ricotta, Parmesan, cream cheese, and cheese wheels)

- Miyoko's Creamery (Mozzarella; Cream Cheese; Cheese Wheels)
- Scratch House Vegan Specialties located in San Diego, California
- Treeline (Soft French-Style Cheeses; Aged Artisanal Cheese Wheels)
- Tofutti (Ricotta)
- Kite Hill (Ricotta)
- Yvonne's Vegan Kitchen (Vegan Goatless Cheese)
- Follow Your Heart (Feta Crumbles)
- Violife (Just Like Feta; Just Like Parmesan)
- Follow Your Heart (Parmesan)

BUTTER

- Miyoko's
- Earth Balance
- Country Crock
- Forager Project

MILK

- Silk (Heavy Whipping Cream; Half-and-Half)
- Ripple (Half-and-Half)

About the Author

Brianna Claxton is the chef and creative force behind PLVNTFOOD, built on the understanding that food is art. While vegan food has, in some circles, inherited the reputation of boring rabbit food, Brianna takes it in the other direction with mind-blowing flavors and possibilities. Her mission is to heal, inspire, tease, delight, and encourage the exploration of new cuisines. Brianna learned to cook from her Italian grandmother and continues to rework, veganize, and refine the recipes that were passed down to her. These family recipes feature an array of colors and textures and often form the centerpiece of a full vegan table.

Brianna has been featured by a variety of outlets and events, including an appearance on Amazon Prime's *High Cuisine* and a signature appearance at Eat Drink Vegan Festival, where Brianna/plvntfood collaborated with Yeastie Boys Bagels for a signature featured dish. She has appeared in or has written for PETA, Mercy for Animals, and *VegNews*.

Index